Startup Selling:

How to sell if you really, really have to and don't know how…

SCOTT SAMBUCCI

Copyright © 2012 Scott Sambucci

All rights reserved.

ISBN-13: 978-1468159240

DEDICATION

To the Entrepreneur – Despite statistical probabilities, you keep going.

To Nikola Tesla – Why did you let Edison out-sell you?

To Lena – Thank you. For everything.

CONTENTS

	Acknowledgments	i
	Introduction	iii
1	Handling Inbound Calls & Leads	1
2	Pick up the Phone	17
3	Find Your Voice	25
4	The Sales Process: Prospecting & New Calls	32
5	Prospecting at Conferences	42
6	More Sales Process	51
7	Build with Value	61
8	Vampires & Gatekeepers	78
9	Revenue Matters	76
10	Negotiation & Contracts	86
11	Be Nice & Eat Your Broccoli	97
12	Love the Grind	103
	About Me	113

ACKNOWLEDGMENTS

Thank you to the authors, mentors, and speakers that helped me develop a sales acumen and self-belief – including Brian Tracy, Zig Ziglar, Neil Rackham, Michael Pedone, Sean Murphy, Peter Cohen, James Altucher, Tony Robbins, and many others. Thank you to those that helped me during key moments of my career – Tom Injaychock for my first internship in college; Rich Gridley for showing me that one can have a career in sales; Butch Porter for many late night strategy calls during my first year; Gary June for telling me that I can be a real pain in the rear; Steve Helba for teaching me the craft of publishing; David Kornacker, Paul Romer, and Sally Elliott for pulling me to Silicon Valley; and Altos Research for one heck of a ride. Thank you to all of my customers throughout the years and for those to come. Thank you to my parents for the lists of chores every day. Now I understand. Lastly, and most importantly, thank you to my wife who supports and endures my quest for everything

Introduction: Why This Book & What to Expect

Why read this book?

- In the next 20 minutes, you might get an inbound phone call or "request for information" email from your website. How are you going to capitalize on that opportunity?
- You have an industry conference in a week that you'd like to attend but you don't have $2500 for the registration fee, and you don't want to stand around talking to other less capable CEOs about their problems. You want real meetings with real outcomes. How will you make this happen?
- You have an attendee list from a previous industry event. Many of the attendees should be using your product. What do you do with it? How do you turn these leads into prospects?
- You're an entrepreneur with a few beta testers and a little bit of revenue (or not), but before you can hire a full-time salesperson, you need to land 3-4 real clients paying you real money. How do you develop these prospects into customers?
- You have very happy beta testers, but they're delaying the part where they actually pay you money. They're really nice engineers, but they keep telling you that the business managers aren't ready to pull the trigger. Closing even one or two of these will be a huge boost to your company, your revenues, and your confidence. How do you get them from "users" to "buyers"?

As I pecked away each morning, I wrote for a technical founder (or team) or a CEO of a young company – someone in alpha or beta stage with a demonstrable product and an idea dripping with potential. While you're sitting at your desk coding or productizing, the phone might ring every so often or you receive an occasional "request for information" email from your website. Perhaps you're lucky enough to gain an introduction from your venture capital partner or friends in the industry.

Your press on TechCrunch isn't bringing in the sales by the thousands like you thought and you've been to a few industry events where potential customers have told you - "Hey, this is interesting, I'd like to know more…" – but you can't seem to pull them into any real sales process. Now you're developing your sales channel.

You might be an engineer turned founder or a product manager that's great at product development or solving really hard technical problems, but selling remains a mystery that you absolutely need to solve. You might have had some customer interactions in the past as a product manager, sales engineer, or marketing person, but you've never really had to sell. You need to add a few clients before you can really go after that big Series A round of funding. Your angels are a little restless, or worse, you don't have angels and your spouse is a little restless.

This book gives you clear and practical advice that you can start using right now. Today. In the next 20 minutes. Take the time to read every chapter. Every chapter. Every single one. As you read each chapter, begin integrating these ideas right away. I promise they will make a difference in your business. You will immediately see how inbound calls respond differently, how you're able to decode the decision process, and how to find the complacent and discontented people in your industry that you set up shop to help in the first place. ("This sure seemed like a good idea…" right?)

This book assumes that you know very little about the structural aspects of sales and the selling process, and provides everyday sales strategies and tactics you can utilize immediately in your business. In fact, words like "sales" and "selling" usually give you the creeps.

v

1 - Handling Inbound Calls & Leads

Sales Tenet #1: For inbound calls and leads, find out why the prospect is inquiring about your products and services.

Sales Tenet #2: Jumping right into a sales demo on the first call is the kiss of death.

Whether you're a start-up or working for an established company, you're promoting your company at various events and through your network. You might have a private beta program established for prospective customers, or fielding a few introductions from your investors. The result is an occasional phone call or email. How do you handle these inbound leads?

Inbound callers will usually start off the conversation with one of these openers:

"I was on your website – can you tell me a more about what you do?"

"I didn't see any pricing on your website – how much is it?"

"I heard about your company and wanted to take a look at your product."

"I was wondering - do you guys have a product that does such-and-such?"

First, before you do anything, resist the temptation to answer their specific question right away. If it's an inbound phone call, immediately get the person's name and ask them to repeat it if you didn't get it this first time. Write it down. People talk fast on the phone and often skip telling you their name. They're not being rude; it's just the way we communicate.

Your first objective is to create a conversation between two people instead of some guy from one company calling some guy at another company to request information. More importantly, you need to take control of the conversation by asking the questions, instead of getting peppered by a stranger. This is very, very important. It slows down the pace of the call and allows you to direct the conversation to the customer's needs based on your product, instead of the other way around. The customer has a very specific problem that they are trying to solve. In fact, it's such a specific problem that they've taken the action of calling you directly. Wow – they must really need help!

Sometimes your specific product or service solves their exact problem, but here's the thing - even if you have the exact solution that they ask about, you don't know *why* they are looking for your thing-a-ma-bob or whatchamacallit. Even if your product solves 90% of that problem and you puke on them with everything about your product, how it's built, and your inspiration for starting the company, it doesn't matter because 90% isn't enough. The caller will almost always object and say - "Yeah, that's almost what I need but I'm looking for such-and-such. Thanks, anyway." Now you're dead. You have to wrestle control of the conversation to help this person discover the answer to their problem.

Think about those old detective shows in which there's an interrogation. The perpetrator tries to take control of the conversation and the cop rebuts with, "I'll ask the questions here." That's because he who asks the questions controls the conversation.

Image: Peter Falk as "Columbo."
http://upload.wikimedia.org/wikipedia/commons/b/bc/Peter_Falk_Richard_Kiley_Colombo_1974.JPG

Why do you ask questions? So that you can determine their specific needs and establish decision criteria. As the conversation develops, you can even begin differentiating your product and company (more advanced sales techniques that we'll cover later). You have to begin by giving your caller something though, and that's where your conversation and transition skills are vital. A good response might be:

> "We sure do. We have a number of different products that can help with that. Tell me a little bit more about [why you're asking/what you're doing] so we can direct you to the right thing-a-ma-bob. Also, I didn't catch your name - what was it?"

Ninety nine percent of the time, they'll open up and say something like:

> "Oh, yeah. I'm Bob Smith calling from XYZ Technology. We're thinking about implementing a new enterprise management system and I read about your company so I figured I'd give you a call."

Now you're in. While he's talking, listen to what he's saying. If you can quickly, and I mean, quickly, pull up their company in your web browser, then do it so have it in front of you. If you cannot do this quickly, don't worry about it. It's waaaaaay more important to listen so you can ask intelligent questions than it is to fumble around with whether his company is XYZ.com or XYZTechnology.com.

After you let him tell you everything and you take control of the conversation by asking questions, be sure to restate your name - he didn't catch it when you answered the phone. Trust me – he didn't. For example:

> "Okay, that makes sense. Thanks for the background. By the way, if you didn't catch it, my name is Scott. [Pause] So I had a question about what you just shared – what's prompting the look at a new enterprise management system [or whatever need they have]?" Now you're in a conversation assessing the person's needs.

Develop some shorthand notation for your note-taking. A pattern of common terms and situations will emerge very quickly. Some examples I use for my notes in my business (housing data):

NF = New Fund

SF/MF = houses/condos

CS = Case-Shiller

INV = Investor

VAL = Valuation Company

Do the same for your business and industry.

A couple of rules for handing inbound calls

1. Be nice. Always, always, always be nice. If you can't be nice at that moment, don't answer the phone.

2. Smile when you talk.
3. Listen to what the prospect is saying and ask for clarification if you're not sure. Ask them to repeat what they just said. It's okay – you're allowed. This will assure you are getting your facts straight and you will appear thoughtful because of your determination to understand the prospect's pain.
4. Ask questions - real questions about the person: how they heard about your company and why they are calling. (More on questions in Chapter 6 – "More Sales Process.")
5. Be succinct. Ask and answer questions clearly, but use not more than three sentences in a row before flipping around the conversation with a question to the prospect. Nobody is ever going to call you because they want to hear a soliloquy. You aren't nearly as interesting as your prospect.

Answer your phone with a warm greeting like, "Good afternoon – this is Scott," or "Good morning! Thanks for calling – this is Scott." Remember, the person on the other end thinks they're calling a real company with a real product. Just because you're answering the call on your cell phone doesn't mean that grunts and garbled greetings are acceptable.

If you're using your cell phone as your main company number or you're forwarding a land line or Skype number to your cell phone, keep a pen and a notebook with you at all times. Personally, I like the top-open variety. Buy ten of these at a time and keep a couple in your car, your sport coat pockets, and next to your wallet and keys at home so that you always have one handy. Keep a pen inserted into the spiral binding with each one too. Keep a decent pen with you at all times – one that writes smoothly so you can jot notes as quickly as the person is talking. Cheap ballpoints from the Days Inn in Omaha, NE that you found at the post office are out of the question.

Example: Inbound call from Lakeland, FL

We had a real estate broker call into our main phone number. He immediately launched into his reason for calling. He was on our website and trying to find a market report for his local town, but his town wasn't showing up on the website. He had visited our website a couple of months ago, but now he wasn't seeing his town listed. Wow - that's a TON of information that he shared without me asking a single question. Here's what I learned even before I said a single word:

1. He was a broker from Coldwell Banker in Lakeland, FL - because my caller ID said so. Of course, he didn't know that I knew that and I wasn't going to play Big Brother and scare him away. But, he was qualified now as a legitimate prospect.
2. He was darn interested based on what he told me; he was on our site a month ago, remembered it and liked it enough to come back, and was interested enough to pick up the phone, suffer through our phone system, dial my extension and wait for it to ring a few times just to find the market report he wanted.
3. I had an opportunity to engage in an action with him that will help us develop rapport; he's on our website and something is not working correctly. I can go into quick customer service mode and with him on the line, see if I see what he's seeing. (See Chapter 7 – "Build with Value" and Chapter 11 – "Be Nice & Eat Your Broccoli.")

I could have used the Lakeland caller ID info and said, "I'm showing an 863 area code. Is that in Florida?" Then, he would have said, "Yes, we're in Lakeland" and been a little spooked. Instead, I went this direction:

Me: "Wow - thanks for calling! I can definitely help out with that. Tell me about yourself. Where are you based? Are you a broker, an agent, or both?"

Him: "I'm an agent down in Lakeland, FL. Well, I'm actually in Winter Haven. If you've never heard of it, it's between Tampa and Orlando."

Me: "Believe it or not, I know it very well. I used to live in Pinellas County and went to high school in Palm Harbor. We used to drive through Lakeland to get to Disney World when we were kids."

Then, we talked for a few minutes about the old Boardwalk & Baseball and Major League Baseball Spring Training facilities that used to be there.

Me: "It's great to talk to someone from down there! So let's get you fixed up with the reports you need." (Note the psychology here - "we" "fixed" "you" "need")

Me: "So, you were at our company home page and typed 'Lakeland FL' into the box and your market didn't show up there?"

Him: "Yep, that's right."

Me: "Okay, I'm going to our website right now." (Then, I typed in Lakeland, Florida and had the same problem - our market didn't show up on our website.)

Me: "Well, the good news is that I'm seeing what you're seeing. Lakeland, Florida isn't showing up. No problem. Here's what we'll do. I'm going to have one of my colleagues here, Katie Harris, help us with this. She can email you a report for Lakeland and talk with you about any questions you have. What's your email address?" I took that down, and repeated it back to him to make sure I had it right.

Me: "Great, and Michael, what's your phone number?" I took that down, and repeated it back to him to make sure I had it right. "I'm going to send you an email and copy Katie, explaining that you need a report..."

Katie followed up with the report and we're now in the sales process with him. Done and done.

Example: Inbound call - Investment Fund

I received another inbound call via our "1-877-xxx-xxxx" line. The call inquired if we had data for the Rental Market.

Me: "Good morning! Altos Research, this is Scott."

Him: "Hi. I was calling to see if you had data on the rental market."

See how he unintentionally laid a trap for me? Our rental data product was brand new at the time. We just did a press release a month prior and this new product surfaced in more than half of our sales calls now. I very, very easily could have responded with an enthusiastic, "Yes we sure do!" to which he would have replied, "Okay great. Tell me about it. How much is it?"

Instead, I followed the prescription above. I answered his question succinctly and then reversed the conversation.

Me: "We sure do, and lots of it (smiling into the phone so he could hear my friendliness). Tell me a little more about your question; what exactly are you looking for?"

He (I'll call him "Jeff" here) was looking for local rental rates over time. There are plenty of public sources in which he was able to view individual rental listings today, but not what rental rates were a year ago. He needed to develop a time series of data to show rental rates over time for specific communities and markets. He concluded his explanation with this question, "Do you have anything like that?"

Me (with a smile into the phone): "That's exactly what we do. Will that be cash, check, or charge?" (Trial close to determine his seriousness.)

Jeff: "Charge probably..." (Bang – we're in.)

Me: "Great. Our rental data is exactly what you just described. We watch the rental markets every week across the entire country and, then, aggregate the rental listings and calculate local statistics by zip code. Our data goes back several years. How much of a time series do you need?" (Repeating the criteria so we're both clear and, then, asking another qualifying question.)

Jeff was new with this fund and has been in the housing industry for about 20 years. He was leading a prospective effort with the fund to examine rental rate changes versus home price changes over same period of time. From here, we engaged in a friendly banter about research ideas and further qualification. He specifically asked, "I'd like to see rental price trends for three bedroom rentals over the past year in Scottsdale, AZ." He's developing an internal presentation, using several markets as case studies. If his hypothesis appears confirmed, his fund will establish a new fund and require housing data for regular surveillance of the fund's assets.

Yes, these are a lot of grueling details about this particular set of needs and applications of the rental data – and that's exactly the point. By tip-toeing around the unintentional trap that Jeff set by his innocuous question "Do you have rental data?" we explored in detail his situation, his criteria, next actions, how our products fit into his work, and most importantly, how the rental data product is going to make Jeff look like a rock star at his internal presentation. He's brand new with the fund. Think that's just a little bit of pressure there? We're helping him fire out of the gate with his new colleagues.

Now that I had a good picture of where Jeff needed to go with the rental data, the final step is setting up our initial product demo (For more on how to lead a killer product demo, see "Great Demo!" by Peter Cohen at www.secondderivative.com/Reading.html). In this next call, I would show our rental data for Scottsdale, AZ trended over the past year with our housing market data.

Remember Sales Tenet #2: Jumping right into a sales demo on the first call is the kiss of death.

Me: "Jeff, here's what I recommend. I can put together an example of our data for Scottsdale and share it with you. How about Wednesday afternoon at the same time, 4 pm Central, for us to hop back on a call and view it together?"

Jeff: "Wednesday at 4 pm. That works perfect. Will you send me a meeting invite?"

Me: "Yep, it will include a link for screen sharing. I'll call your office line. What's that number?"

Jeff: "It's (555) XXX-XXXX."

Me: "Great, that's (555) XXX-XXXX, correct?"

Jeff: "You got it."

Me: "And what's your email address?"

Jeff: "It's Jeff Smith (one word) spelled G-E-O-F-F-S-M-I-T-H at bighedgefund dot com."

Me: "Got it; that's G-E-O-F-F-S-M-I-T-H at bighedgefund dot com."

(His name really wasn't Geoff and he didn't have an unusual spelling to his name. I added this to this example to illustrate the point – always, always, always confirm the information you are recording. It is too easy to transpose numbers or misspell names. "Greg" vs. "Gregg" and "Kristine" vs. "Christine.)

After the call, here are the immediate steps I took:

1. <u>Sent the meeting invite.</u> Google calendar rocks. I included a clear explanation of the meeting and objective, and included a reminder email. Remember, Geoff is a busy guy. He needs to see his calendar every day and remember EXACTLY why he has this time booked with you or you introduce the risk of a blow-off regardless of how interested Geoff may seem on this inbound call.

Calendar Event

Rental data review (Altos Research) Geoff Smith/Scott Saml

- 12/21/2011 2:00pm to 2:30pm 12/21/2011 Time zone
- All day / Repeat
- **Event details** / Find a time
- **Where:** Scott to call Geoff at (555) XXX-XXX / map
- **Calendar:** Scott Sambucci
- **Description:** Viewing rental data examples from Scottsdale, AZ. Scott to share his screen using: https://join.me/ Please click this link.
- **Attachment:** Add attachment
- **Event color:** ▪
- **Reminders:** Pop-up 10 minutes × / Email 10 minutes × / Add a reminder

2. <u>Searched for Geoff on LinkedIn</u>. I want to know more about him for the next call, his background, previous employers, and where he studied. All of this adds to my fundamental understanding of Geoff and offers an opportunity to ask more questions about him.

3. <u>Added Geoff to my CRM</u>, including all of his contact information, his LinkedIn profile, and added him to our monthly marketing drip.

Advanced Example: Inbound email & phone call - Investment Fund

We received this inbound email:

> *I'm interested to take a premium subscription for the counties San Francisco, CA, Manhattan County, NY, Hudson County, NJ and Suffolk County, MA. However before making any payments, I want to be sure of exactly what information we will have access to.*

> *We are looking to get hold of very in depth research in specific areas of these counties. For example we want to be able to see what recent sales there have been in downtown Manhattan for a particular condominium size and what rent can be expected to be achieved for these condominium sizes in the financial district.*

> *I noticed you have price trends graphs for the whole county but do you have data which would allow us to break this down to specific neighbourhoods in the county? For example SOMA in San Francisco or Jersey City in Hudson County?*
>
> *If you could provide me with example data you provide or if we could have a remote online run through that would be great.*

This is an inbound lead from a fund located overseas (Southeast Asia). We don't get too many international leads and the obvious time difference makes a call back squirrelly. The email is very specific and a delightful one to receive. The prospect has given us a huge amount of information. They:

- Spent time on our website.
- Gave us an idea of how much data they need – a specific number of metros and markets instead of the entire country, plus telling us at what geographic level they need data. In this case, it's micro-market data (i.e. the SOMA neighborhood in San Francisco).
- Asked about "recent sales" and rental rates. We have rental data, but not "recent sales."
- We're open to a phone call.

Here are the actions that would cause you to fall into the lazy man's trap:

1. You could respond to his specific questions in an email. "We have rental data, though we can't help you with the recent sales."
2. You reply back and say, "Great! Here are a few files to check out," and then email a bunch of data files that won't make sense.
3. Set up a call and then jump right into a demo of the data and tools that we have.

On the surface, this seems like an easy one, but as Butch Porter, my first sales manager affectionately told me, "There's a million ways to f&*K up a sale." Our rep went the email route. He acknowledged receipt and immediately prompted for a phone call. (Looking back, I would have preferred our sales rep respond with a phone call instead of an email. See Chapter 2 – "Pick up the Phone." Sometimes inbound emails do not include phone numbers of the sender, so you're stuck with no choice but to reply electronically.) His reply:

> *I'd be more than happy to answer your questions regarding your real estate data needs. I am located in California (Pacific Standard Time) so please let me know when you could jump on a phone call!*

The prospect replied back quickly to our returned email and we established a call time and sent a meeting invite. We DID NOT include web meeting or screen-sharing information in the meeting invite – this was intentionally going to be a phone call only so that we could ask questions to identify specific prospects needs and develop an organized sales process.

To do so in this case, or any case, you must implement a questioning framework. A questioning framework creates a structure around your communication and interaction with your prospect, enabling you to control the conversation and identify opportunities for your product to solve the prospect's core business issue. I recommend using the "SPIN" framework - Situation, Problem, Implication, Need-Payoff ("SPIN Selling" by Neil Rackham. McGraw-Hill, 1988):

- Situation questions gather background information and develop understanding of the context of the sale. Examples:
    - "What enterprise software solution do you use currently?"
    - "How many users of your existing platform are in your company?"
    - "When was the last time that you integrated a new enterprise software solution?"
    - "Do you host your current product locally, or is it cloud-based?"
- Problem questions prod at customer problems, dissatisfactions, or short-comings with their existing process. Example:
    - "If your current enterprise software only enables you to enter data into the system but not export it, how does that affect the work flow of your team?"
    - "Because you're hosting your current product in use locally, what sort of headaches does that cause for your IT team?"
- Implication questions identify and isolate specific problems with their current process, products, and vendors. These questions set up the Need-Payoff questions where your product solves the problems you've help the prospect identify. Examples:
    - "If your IT team is pushing back on requests that you make to upgrade the system or export the data, what sort of time costs does that create for your sales team?"
    - "If you're not able to export your data, are there situations in which you feel that your team is missing key information for their daily work decisions?"

- Need-Payoff questions uncover the value and ability of your product to solve the implied need you've now established with the prospect. Example:
    - "By making your data exportable from your enterprise software solutions, how much would that increase productivity and avoid poor decisions for your team?"
        → **IMPORTANT NOTE**: It is unlikely that you will be able to walk through this entire questioning framework in a single call. You'll find that your questions will be more oriented around "Situation" and "Problem" at first. Only later in subsequent calls will you be able to decipher what "Implication" and "Need-Payoff" questions to ask.

Your goal in using this framework is to develop a clear structure around your interaction with your prospects. By using SPIN, you will identify yourself as a professional to your prospect, while uncovering the precise reasons for their interest in your product.

Now, back to our Asian fund…. In this case, we set up a phone call to discuss their data needs. Then, we prepared a series of "Situation" questions that will be crucial to learn about their business needs and how our products will fill those needs:

1. Is this fund currently investing in properties, or are they a research team that feeds data and intelligence to other parts of the company?
2. Do they have an active fund now, or are they starting a fund?
3. Why did they ask specifically for "recent sales" and rental data? Ninety percent of our inbound leads ask for a specific product, but they really just need a solution to their problem.

On the call, we asked them:

1. "What type of analysis are you doing?" They told us that what they were up to.
2. "How are you going about your research and analysis now?"

It turned out that they were currently using a consumer website to look at rental data, and the Case-Shiller Home Price Index for housing data. They asked as they closed their explanation, "So, how are you guys different?"

Bingo. Now that I knew the Situation (in part that is, because you will never know the entire customer situation out of the gate; there will

ALWAYS be more that you will discover as you spend more time with prospects. See Chapter 6 – "More Sales Process."), we now had a place to begin our Problem, Implication, and Need-Payoff questions while establishing differentiation of our product compared to their current resources (referring again to the SPIN Selling formula).

> Me: "Here's how we're different. The consumer website you mentioned is just that, a consumer website, which makes access to the underlying data difficult for analytical purposes like you described. If you're doing any sort of heavy spreadsheet analysis or modeling, the data becomes unusable because they only display the data in online charts and graphs. Case-Shiller is an excellent indicator of the housing market. However, we often hear the frustration with the fact that it lags the market by two months and is only available at the metropolitan level. You can't get micro-level data, by zip code or community, like that type you need for your local analysis."

(Admission: I jumped in a little quick and made the assumption that these were our differentiating factors. Fortunately, they immediately agreed with an emphatic "Yes!" so I knew we have our selling position set.)

Now, there's a second trap, jumping right into a demo. In their email, we knew they had specific markets (NYC, Jersey City, San Francisco) and specific data types, recent sales and rental data. We could have queued up that data before the sales call and had it ready to show. In this initial call, we could have powered through these SPIN questions and said, "OK, I think I've got it. Let me show you my screen," and launched a GoToMeeting or Join.me on the fly. The correct way to handle this is to hold off and set another time to talk with the prospect, unless you discover that there is a very specific time constraint for their decision process. If you're selling enterprise software, software-as-a-service, data-as-a-service, or any type of business-to-business solution, the initial call is just that, an initial call. This will be a protracted sales process. You are not going to sell $100,000 enterprise software package over the phone during an initial inbound phone call. By establishing a clear process, you'll be in control of the conversation and pace of the relationship.

I know you have a tremendous fear out that if you let the prospect go without a demo on that initial call, they'll never come back. Here are a couple of truths:

1. If they demand a demo right away, then you haven't developed the correct level of rapport, shown them the level of your professionalism, and relayed importance of your product.

2. You have to take the lead in the conversation. In this case, we had very affable prospects; they were inquisitive and interested, and were willing to take our lead.

3. If they blow off or miss the second call, they weren't a real lead anyway. They were just browsing. Of course, you absolutely want to turn browsers into buyers by establishing an immediate need using good questions. However, if you can't get there, or they're not a willing participant, then let the browser browse, be nice, and then give them a call in a week with: "I was thinking about our conversation and I had a couple of ideas based on an article I just read" approach. (See Chapter 2 – "Pick up the Phone" and Chapter 3 - "Find Your Voice") Totally legitimate. This gives you a chance to reset the conversation and more importantly, take the lead back in the relationship instead of letting them push you around.

The demo call should be a quick turnaround. It can even be the same day if you can put together an effective custom demo for the prospect. In our case, we wanted to export data files for these markets and clean up the data files into a pretty spreadsheet. We asked them for the same time two days later.

A Note on Establishing Rapport

As we started our conversation on the demo call with our Hong Kong prospect two days later, I opened the conversation with, "I was checking out your LinkedIn profile. Looks like you're from Boston." This is a wonderfully effective question, especially for me because I'm an East Coaster from the Philadelphia area. Philadelphia and Boston people have an odd ability to understand each other. Maybe it's the weather, the grind, or being long-suffering sports fans. I know that I can most engage anyone from Boston and develop a connection.

He said he's not from Boston, but spent about five years there. The rest of the conversation:

Him: "I'm originally from New York. You?"

Me: "Jersey." (With a wry smile that I knew he could hear over the phone)

Him: "What part, North Jersey, South Jersey?"

Me: "South Jersey near Philly." (Again with a smile)

Him: "That's cool. My parents go down to this little town on the Jersey Shore called Ocean City."

Me: "You've got to be kidding me. I'm flying to Ocean City

tomorrow for Christmas. My parents just retired. They've had a little beach house down there for 20 years."

We chatted some more about local pizza joints, the boardwalk, and salt water taffy. True story. And all because I asked him about himself (See: "How to Win Friends and Influence People" by Dale Carnegie). And when was in Ocean City, I bought a box of salt water taffies and sent to him.

These guys are now customers.

What about the "No-Talkers" and "How much is it?"

For the 1% that ardently resist your attempt to engage in a conversation - "Just tell me if you have that product" - remember to be nice and smile, and then tell them, "Yep we sure do." Then, they might ask, "How much is it?"

In my company's case, the answer is always "it depends" because it really does. I tell people that: "It depends. We have some clients that pay us more than $200,000 a year and others that pay $200 a month. Everyone is different. Can you tell me a little more about what you're doing so I can give you a more specific answer?" (I start with the $200,000 number to set a high anchor price in case it is a very large fund. We get many random inbound calls ranging from research analysts at billion dollar hedge funds to individual investors buying 1-2 properties at a time. If I go the other way – "We have some clients that pay us $200 a month and others that pay $200,000 a year." – the big funds will immediately begin thinking about how they can get off cheaply.)

In this case, you're using their frame of reference to lead them to where you really want to go, learning about their business and needs. They want to know pricing, so use that as the carrot to get them to where you need to go.

They may ask, "Can you just send me a price sheet?" Be nice. Smile. Then, tell them, "We don't have a price sheet because of all of the iterations of customers and products we have, plus the custom work we do for clients. What sort of work do you do? What is your primary industry focus?" By offering choices, now you are forcing them to think about who they are, or aren't, and in most cases this will prompt them to reply with something like, "We're an online retailer for used bicycle parts." This is far more information than someone calling with the first words, "I was on your website – how much is your software?"

Take the conversation down this path until you get something you can latch onto for a more robust conversation to assess their needs and establish their buying criteria. Ninety percent of the time, this will work with the 1% that are difficult. For the rest, just let them go. They're not worth it right now. Get their email address and send them some basic information on pricing without getting specific, and add them to your marketing drip.

Remember:

Sales Tenet #1: For inbound calls and leads, find out why the prospect is inquiring about your product and has interest in your service.

Sales Tenet #2: Jumping right into a sales demo on the first call is the kiss of death.

2 - Pick up the Phone

Sales Tenet #3: Use the telephone as the default mode of communication.

Several years ago, I worked in a commercial real estate office in downtown San Francisco. There were four senior brokers, each had their own personality and style. The most successful broker had his cubicle in the back right corner. He was there every morning when I arrived at 8am and was already on the phone by then. On a slow day, he probably made 40 phone calls. On a slow day. One after the other. It sounded like he knew every person he called for ten years, and every call had a purpose ranging from finalizing contract details to calling contacts that still had three years remaining on their lease with a competing brokerage.

After a six-month consulting stint, I thought about going full-time in the office, so I sat down with this broker to ask him if he thought I'd be successful. He asked me – "Do you know the most distinguishing trait your have?" I went through the normal list – determination, hard work, organization. He answered – "Your voice. Your voice is perfect for the phone."

Now I don't know if he was talking to me individually, or simply telling me – "Listen – if you want to be successful, you need to pick up the phone." This guy was generally a luddite – I don't think he really knew how to use email and I know he didn't know how to use the fax machine and copier. Yet it didn't matter – it was all about the phone and building personal relationships.

You should use email – it's efficient for sharing information and managing projects, but when you are developing a prospect and a relationship, use every single opportunity you can to PICK UP THE PHONE.

Handling an Inbound Lead

Image: http://upload.wikimedia.org/wikipedia/commons/8/8d/CandlestickTelephoneGal.jpg

I received this email from a person I'd been contacting for about a year:

Hi Scott,

I won't be attending the ASF conference this year, but there is some renewed interest on the team at looking at aggregated data. We are currently reviewing statistics versus HPI data we subscribe to for several vendors. Is there a chance you could provide whatever zip code data you have available for 93550 for review with whatever history you are comfortable providing? We are reviewing the full history for this zip code versus HPI to help us determine whether the data is worthwhile for our broader investment platform.

Thanks,

XXXXX

Even though the email is extremely specific, it's vital to understand why they are reviewing the data they are receiving from their current vendors. This will establish their buying criteria.

So, what you do here? PICK UP THE PHONE. This allowed me to ask "Situation" questions and begin establishing decision criteria.

This email was the start of a six-month sales process that ended up with this prospect becoming a very large customer. What if I would have just emailed back with a sample data file from this zip code? The prospect would have had no idea what they were viewing and as a result, would have made assumptions. He could have taken four minutes to review it and said, "Oh well, not what we needed." By having a conversation and asking "Situation" questions, I learned and developed the criteria for their decision. PICK UP THE PHONE.

Using Minutiae to Build Rapport

In a recent sales interview, we executed a Situational call extremely well. We had the COO and two product managers on the phone. The agreed-upon next step was a review of a property portfolio that the prospect would supply to us by Friday, indicating clear interest because they agreed to do some work and they did it.

However, the property list was cut and pasted into an email - we prefer to receive files in Excel or .CSV file because reduces the administrative work on our end. This is not a big deal, but a nice-to-have as it saves us 15-20 minutes and enables us to start training the prospective early in the process about how our systems work with file formats and the order of column headings. The easiest option was an email reply, "Thanks for sending. Do you have this in an Excel file?" But, what's the problem with this?

1. It makes us look lazy or that we're appending requirements to the test file.
2. The sample file was sent on Friday, just before a long holiday weekend. If we send an email, they might not get the email before the weekend, in which case we burn a few days turning this around. We want to keep the momentum going on this opportunity.

The solution? PICK UP THE PHONE. What does this accomplish?

1. Uncovers additional decision criteria. We've only had the one call so far. Whether your prospect realizes it or not, they are still developing the criteria around which their decision will be made and haven't told you the whole story. A second call offers this opportunity.

    → **IMPORTANT NOTE:** The decision criteria is a formative process, always requiring multiple customer interactions to determine. (See Chapter 6 – "More Sales Process")

2. Differentiates you and trains your customer. Everyone is bombarded with email. If you get in the habit of talking on the phone with a prospect early in the process, they'll then expect it from you and will take your calls every time. If they've been taking your calls consistently throughout the sales process, it will also be more difficult for them to screen or avoid your calls when you reach a low point during the ebb and flow of the sales process. If they do start screening, then you have a clear signal that's something's going horribly wrong in the sales process.

3. Grows the personal relationship. We can have another conversation with the prospect, an opportunity to further the relationship. We've only had the one call with this company. It was productive and concluded with an advance, and both sides were professionally engaged and interested in each other. However, we

didn't get personal enough to begin constructing the peer-to-peer relationship. A phone call in this scenario offers the opportunity to do this, chatting about the holidays, the long weekend, or plans for New Year's Eve.

4. Facilitates visualization product usage. We know they have some urgency in filling this need and how they envision using it because we asked the question - "How do you see yourself using this data?" – during the initial call. A second call will inevitably offer the opportunity for you to confirm what your prospect shared with you in their answer during the first call. "Tell me again, how do you see yourself using this data?" or "You mentioned that you saw yourself using this data for such-and-such reason. Were there any other places where it might fit?" Yes, it is completely legitimate to ask the same question again. You are helping the prospect solve a very hard problem with your product or service. This should not and cannot be taken lightly. To be a true professional, recapping information is an excellent way to show that you are focused on helping the prospect solve their very hard problem.

Ultimately, the result of this call about the file submission enabled our sales rep to learn about the number of portfolios that the customer was managing. More volume means greater need for automation and analysis. Now we knew volume, which emphasized the prospect's needs and gave us the chance to think through pricing options well in advance of that eventual piece of the conversation. Our rep ended up doing the manual cut and paste for the customer, which still accomplished the objective of training the customer – "When you're working with your online account, you'll be uploading a .CSV file of your properties."

Using Minutiae to Build Rapport II

Our same sales rep was working a pretty large deal with a new customer. We went through four or five calls and our initial product demo to set the course of the opportunity and establish the criteria. The two main contacts with the prospective client were in two different cities and time zones. Add in my time to sit in on the sales calls, and we're juggling four schedules to identify a time for the next conversation. Naturally our rep was having some difficulty finding a time. He asked me, "What should I do?" I answered, "PICK UP THE PHONE."

He did, and fifteen minutes later grabbed me to tell me how great the call went. They ended up talking about coffee and personal fitness training, and set a time for the next call. Now, he had more relationship capital with the prospect. Simple - PICK UP THE PHONE.

Example: The Daily Call

Working with a billion dollar hedge fund last year, our sales rep became so intertwined with the project leader at the prospect's company that he was calling every day as the decision day loomed to answer the prospect's questions and check on the project's status. Even after working with them for nearly four months through the sales process, the prospect's team was still identifying criteria based on the products and services available to them from various vendors. After our rep called the prospect's project leader on Wednesday skipping a day on Tuesday, the project leader said, "What happened? I missed my daily call from you yesterday!" He was joking, sort of, and that's the point - the relationship was that strong. And yes, we got the business. They immediately became one of our biggest clients. PICK UP THE PHONE.

Use the News

Here's a little secret – you're allowed to talk to your prospects about more than just your product and their requirements. Be human. (See Chapter 3 – "Find Your Voice".) As you find new information about the industry, think about the secondary and tertiary effects to the market, your clients, and prospects.

Be smart about this. In our industry, there are very public announcements from various home price indices. Everyone sees these and reads them. Even better, look for the nooks and crannies of information, material that your very busy prospect hasn't had a chance to read. Alternately, use the headlines and ask your prospects this question:

> "How does this affect your business?"

This shows genuine interest on your behalf for their business and you will learn all kinds of information that would never surface in a sales call.

Example: Use the News

Here's an example from my industry. (Pay no attention to the specifics of my industry here. Just focus on the outcome.) A "Too Big to Fail" bank (TBTF) announced that they were experimenting with REO Sales in managing their distressed mortgage portfolio. This was potentially a very big opportunity for the distressed investment funds in the market, because it presented a slew of new products for them to purchase. I made four phone calls that afternoon, three to existing clients and one to a prospective client, to ask them "How does this affect your business?" I got voicemail for the three clients.

<u>Prospective Client</u>: Picked up the phone.

Me: "Hi _____ - Scott Sambucci over at Altos Research. Got a minute?"

Prospect: "Yeah, actually I do. What's up?"

Bingo - I'm in. I asked about the REO program and how it might affect his business. He didn't even know about the TBTF REO sale program and said that this was exactly in their sweet spot for their investment fund. I learned a number of new aspects about his company. They have several verticals, including one that focuses on REO asset disposition and property preservation. I told him about another one of our clients focusing on REO purchases, that they were contracting with a company I knew that company also does property preservation services. "Yeah, they're one of our competitors." New information.

We talked more about the distressed asset market more generally. I learned that many times banks combine non-performing notes with REOs in the same pool, so this prospect's company likes to co-bid with other firms and then they split out the pool based on the assets they want respectively. Bingo. Now, this is a chance for me to add value to both this prospective company and the aforementioned client by putting them together. Our other client is focusing only on specific geographic markets, so this could be an ideal situation for them to access product in pools where they would be individually blocked because they might include notes or properties in markets outside of their focus. That's real information for both sides because I chose to PICK UP THE PHONE.

For the other three calls in which I left voicemails:

Existing Client #1: My voicemail was specific and to the point, that I read the TBTF announcement, that I remembered that this bank was a client of theirs, and I thought this new initiative might impact their business. Then, I sent an email following the voicemail. The client replied to my email with his thoughts and perspectives on the announcement, and asked me if I was planning to attend the upcoming conference and he proposed that we get together there. Bingo. This client has been particularly valuable as they were early adopters of a product we launched last year, patiently working through several technical issues with us.

Existing Client #2: He called me back and the conversation started: "Things are good - we're doing a lot on the REO side, and I don't know if you saw the news, but we just got a big investment to help us develop the mortgage side of the business." He shared that their mortgage platform business is going well and off we went on the conversation. We talked about TBTF's pilot program on REO disposition and I got his opinion on that. I shared a few other opinions that I'd picked up over the last week from other people. This showed my creditability in the market and my sincere interest in the market and industry.

As we talked more, he shared that his company was in the final round of vendors to be selected by TBTF for REO disposition. They are currently managing thousands of these properties for them every month. As we talked through this process, we uncovered that our company could significantly improve their process with our data. New sales opportunity! (Within an hour after the call, he sent me sample portfolio for me to show him how it works. He showed me he's serious by reciprocating with doing some work. It's not just all on me to pull, pull, pull - it's collaborative.)

When we were wrapping up the call, he mentioned a new company that recently formed as a possible buyer of our data. Free referral! I told him about a client of ours based near him that has a business model that he'd be interested in hearing about, so I'm setting up that introduction.

How did all of this come about? Because I thought to pick up the phone based on the news headlines. PICK UP THE PHONE.

Client #3: Never heard back from him. Three out of four ain't too shabby.

Use the news as a reason to PICK UP THE PHONE.

Billing Issues

We picked up a new customer that was building a set of our technology tools into their new product. In short, they became a value-added reseller (VAR) of our products.

It was a start-up product line for them and they wanted a flexible payment schedule. We reached an agreement quickly and set up their account. We usually set up payment on a forward basis due on receipt - customers pay for September's services on September 1, not at of the end of the month in arrears. This customer wanted to pay in arrears. Okay, no problem - 30 days is no big deal. We sent the invoice at the end of September due on receipt. The end of October came and went, and by November 1, we'd been working with the customer and supporting them for two months without payment.

Our rep asked me what we should do. I think you know the answer by now – PICK UP THE PHONE.

So he did. It took a couple of voicemails and a bit of email banter. The customer finally returned our rep's contact attempts. It turns out the customer *assumed* 30-day net terms, for the September invoice which was already billed in arrears by 30 days. Our rep politely explained that our billing is due on receipt and we've already extended payment a month, a decision that was particularly risky for us, given that the prospect's company was a start-up and we've been fronting engineering time and support for the account. The customer wasn't very happy to hear this initially, but the more they talked, the more the customer understood. He sent the September payment that week. We received the October payment in mid-December - much better.

There is no way this type of understanding happens over email. Imagine if we went the email route going back and forth and back and forth trying to explain our billing policy. The customer would be reading emails from us about payment and billing, asking himself, "Why are these guys so difficult to work with? I sent the payment 30 days after receiving the invoice like I do with all of my other vendors. Maybe I need to find another option for this part of my platform." We circumvented all of this because we chose to PICK UP THE PHONE. (See more about billing issues in Chapter 9 – "Revenue Matters".)

Leaving Voicemails

Michael Pedone at Salesbuzz.com is the man. Spend thirty minutes and listen to this recorded webinar (it's free!):

www.salesbuzz.com/free-demo/voicemail-strategies.aspx

He covers everything you need to know. I've listened and re-listened to many of his recordings. There's no one better in the business when it comes to phone sales and concepts.

Remember:

Sales Tenet #3: Use the telephone as the default communication mode.

Sales Tenet #4: The decision criteria is a formative process, always requiring multiple customer interactions to determine.

3 - Find Your Voice

Sales Tenet #4: Speak human.

Your voice follows you everywhere, your phone calls, your emails, your company website, your blog, Twitter, and LinkedIn. Find your voice to build loyalty and expertise by being personal and speaking human, wherever and whenever you have the opportunity to do so.

Photo by Pirlouiiiit from Marseille, France (crop of Stade_Pavarotti_2b) [CC-BY-SA-2.0 (www.creativecommons.org/licenses/by-sa/2.0)], via Wikimedia Commons (http://en.wikipedia.org/wiki/File:Luciano_Pavarotti_15.06.02_cropped2.jpg)

Breaking down the walls on the phone

When you're waiting on the phone to start a phone demo of your product, never, ever ask, "So, how's the weather out there?" First of all, chances are that it's either too hot, too cold, or really, really nice and the person wishes they were anywhere else other than in their cubicle talking to you. Secondly, you can check the weather, if you really want to know.

Here's a thought: go to their LinkedIn profile and ask them something specific about themselves. People are darn proud of their accomplishments and relish when people ask them something about them. For example, I just randomly pulled up the LinkedIn profile for one of my contacts. He went to Humboldt State University for his undergraduate degree, and then immediately went to the University of Arizona for his Masters degree. That's a big change. Next time I talk to him, I'm asking him:

> "Hi ____, I was checking out your LinkedIn profile. I didn't know you went to Humboldt State. Then, you went right to Tucson. How was that? Must have been quite a change."

Here's another example: a Wall Street contact went to high school and college in Wisconsin, and then his first job out of school was in Wisconsin -

> "Hi _____. You know, I never realized that you were from Wisconsin. I saw that you went to University of Wisconsin-Lacrosse and your first job out of school was in Madison. I'm an East Coaster. What was it like growing up there?"

Next, learn the transition from the niceties to the business conversation without a structural break in your tone and demeanor. Otherwise, your questions about them will immediately seem insincere. Something like:

> "Wow, that's really interesting. I visited Appleton for a friend's wedding and traveled to Milwaukee for business a few times, but I've never spent any real time in upstate Wisconsin. I was just looking at our market data for Madison; it looks like it's a pretty stable market overall. Maybe it's the university that keeps demand somewhat steady?"

Now you've transitioned into the business conversation. You might let him run a bit if he wants to talk more about Wisconsin - that's okay. You've introduced the business lightly to him and then you can say something like:

> "That's pretty neat. I'm not sure if any of the loans you sent to us are in Wisconsin, but let's take a look."

When you are calling in to your leads and prospects, be friendly, be professional, and be human. Have a conversation; don't talk in sales speak. It's not your words that sell. It's your preparation, your questions, your comprehension of the prospect's problems, and your actions to solve them. Yes, you need to talk about the product and talk about their business, but you have to do it in a comfortable way. If you talk in sales speak, your prospects will feel like they're getting pitched. This is particularly important when you have a scheduled call or web meeting for a product demo. Your prospects will instinctively bait you into pitching.

For example, here's a typical start to a web meeting once all of the attendees have arrived:

You: "So should we get started?"

Prospect: "Yep, I'm all ears. Fire away with your pitch. Should I be seeing a PowerPoint slide or something on my screen?"

Your first instinct from the sales side is to acquiesce to the prospects expectations to "hear a pitch." You must resist. If you hear this from your prospect, then:

You: "A pitch? Hmmm... (with a smile of course). Well, I was more prepared for a conversation we'd have as we go along. We're both going to have questions for each other, so I expect you'll be doing as much talking as me so we can take our walk-through in the direction that suits your situation best."

Now you've altered the path and developed a unique voice for yourself in the way you demonstrate your product, not to mention that an interactive conversation is the one way to develop the prospect and define his decision criteria.

Send Thank You cards

As a textbook sales representative with Prentice Hall, I wrote out up to 50-60 of these every Saturday morning, one for everyone I met in person that week. The cards where custom postcards that I had printed at OfficeMax with the company logo, my return address, and the heading "Just A Note...". The notes I mailed were simple:

Dr. Brown - Thank you for your time on Tuesday. As promised, I've ordered a review copy of Dessler's "Human Resource Management" for you. I'll be visiting your department in about two weeks and will be sure to stop by to get your thoughts.

Talk to you then!

-Scott Sambucci

I also used these cards when I stopped by a professor's office and they weren't there. I'd slip one under the door -

Dr. Smith - Sorry to miss you today. You should have received your copy of Freeman's "Anatomy & Physiology" that I ordered after my last visit. I'll send you an email tonight and perhaps we can find a time to chat on the phone.

Thanks!

-Scott Sambucci

The most rewarding moment came when I bumped into a competing sales representative in the halls of UNC-Charlotte's Business School one day. We were chatting and she saw my stack of empty cards in my bag's side pouch. The competing rep said, "Just a note. (in a mimicking voice) I see those things everywhere!" Exactly. It would have been just as easy for her to do them. But she didn't. And that's the point. Take an extra 60 seconds to handwrite a note and send it. You can buy a box of 50 'Thank You' cards for $5.00 at WalMart. If you want to splurge, go to a local stationary store or go to Zazzle.com and have custom ones printed up with your logo and shipped to your door. Absolutely, have these professionally printed. Print them on nice card stock. Do not print them at home with a laser printer. It'll cost you less than $100 to have a huge stack.

More recently, I sat down after an industry conference this Fall. Over three days, I visited, talked, and met with about 40 people. When I got back to the office, I blocked out a morning and wrote out thank you cards to every single person and mailed them. A week later, I received a voicemail from my main contact at a very large investment fund that I'd been working for more than ten months:

> *"Scott hi, this is _____ from _____ and thanks for much for your card. It is the one and only handwritten thank you note I received from the conference. It's so unique. But that's not why I'm calling. I wanted to just refresh my memory about what you know sort of ball park bare bones pricing and service would be. I can describe to you what our immediate need is and I think that you know we would benefit from more than we have immediately and so I just wanted to get some idea of pricing and packages. If you can give me a call back on XXX-XXX-XXXX. Thanks. Bye"*

The only handwritten note he received. I still smile about that.

Here's another example from my interaction with a sales representative at a prospective client:

I was developing a very good relationship with the senior managers as they were pushing through the sales process. The managers kindly invited me to a closed dinner with their clients, so that I could get to know the company some more as part of the work we'd been discussing. This prospective client was developing a new product package that would include our services as part of the product suite, a huge differentiator in their otherwise commoditized market. Their sales representative would be selling this package to their end clients.

We met at the dinner, but things were a little cold. Rightfully so, as she didn't really know who I was or why some other salesperson from another company was at their dinner. After the conference, I sent her a simple note thanking her for the conversation. A week later, she greeted me warmly in an email:

Scott,

First, thank you for the very nice thank you note! It was a pleasure also to meet you.

Second, I saw you are going to the _____ event next week in _____. When do you get in? We are sponsoring a dinner Saturday night and sent you an invite. You may not get in until Sunday. Do you want to also try to get together on Monday for coffee? I guess I need to find out if _____ is going....if so, then maybe we can all do dinner Sunday night.

Thanks,

Did I misread the frostiness at dinner? Sure I did. She was probably pretty stressed out in a room full of clients having dinner with her managers and the company's CEO. But with the thank you card, I was in for sure.

→ **IMPORTANT NOTE**: People that think your thank you cards are cheesy or silly are not nice people. You don't want to work with them anyway. Move on.

Example: Onsite Workshop

With a very large investor client, after establishing the first-level relationship and establishing them as clients, we reached a more direct level in the relationship. Phone calls were collaborative. They asked me questions. I asked them questions. We were on the same team. I also made it a point to meet and talk with as many people at their company as I could. In July, I was at an academic conference where I met with a senior manager in another division. We chatted and had a very pleasant conversation. (Yes, I sent him a thank you note afterwards.)

It turned out that this person organizes monthly workshops at which key managers from every division meet together for a presentation. That collaboration led to an invitation to present to 30+ of the smartest people at the company. One person kept peppering me with questions, especially about one of our data sets. They were really good questions, very precise and fair. I think I answered them in a clear, direct way, but spoke candidly and humanly. Later at lunch, my main contact at the account said, "Oh yeah. That guy asking all the questions was our chief economist." Oh. Thanks for letting me know.

Two months later, I received an unsolicited email from the workshop organizer to ask me about our new product. He's on an Advisory Committee to review these products. I talked with him about his requirements and then called my main contact to discuss next steps. In the course of this conversation, my main contact explained how he's been cleared to hire eight new people and needs consulting help. We do that, too. Our onsite meeting is set up for later this month.

By developing a voice and a relationship, I got to a point where I had access to the most senior managers and the entire modeling team to discuss implementation and uses of our products, and the opportunity to introduce them to a new product we were rolling out later that year.

Cheekiness

One step beyond "speaking human" is "cheekiness." If you can get cheeky with your customers and contacts, and it flows naturally, then you've developed a unique voice. Here's an example of a LinkedIn message I sent to a prospect that we got to know pretty well throughout the sales process. The process stalled a little when we got to the contract phase. Both sides awaited their legal team's review of the licensing agreement (See Chapter 11 – "Negotiation & Contracts"). I thought I'd try to motivate the prospect to overcome this hurdle with some cheekiness:

> *Hi _____ - Thanks for accepting my invitation to connect here on LinkedIn.*
>
> *John forwarded me the email you sent over - we're ready to get started when you are.*
>
> *But just so you know, I told John (our sales rep) that he's not allowed to leave the office until we have the agreement finished. You should see him. He hasn't shaved in more than 12 days and his clothes are wearing thin. I brought him a change of socks the other day because it was getting pretty bad.*
>
> *The good news is that the HVAC is coming to fix the heat soon, so at least he won't be cold sleeping under his desk at night now. And he can do all of his Christmas shopping online.*
>
> *Talk soon,*
>
> *-Scott S.*

The contract's still taken longer to finalize than we'd like, but the point is that we reached a point in our working relationship where I felt comfortable sending this note to him. He laughed about it.

Find your voice.

Social Platforms

I absolutely, positively recommend choosing 2-3 media platforms and becoming active. Personally, I use our company blog, a personal blog, Twitter, and LinkedIn. The blogs enable me to share perspectives and industry expertise in detail, while Twitter and LinkedIn allow for sharing these posts and for daily interactions with customers.

I post links to my blog posts on my LinkedIn Profile page, so that anyone the finds me on LinkedIn (your prospects and customers will Google stalk you), can learn more about me beyond my online resume.

Groups on LinkedIn can be effective, but often get spammy very quickly so be careful spending too much time on these. That said, one of our sales reps set up a group, "Residential Mortgage Backed Securities (RMBS)." Given that many of our contacts in the industry use LinkedIn for their resumes, I was surprised to see that this particular group had not yet been established. We now have 375+ members in the group. For an upcoming industry conference, I posted a quick thought to facilitate interaction:

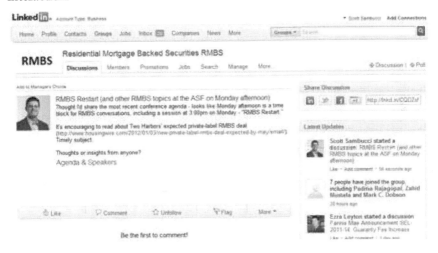

This sort of work only takes a few minutes once you get in the flow and now we have 375+ people in the RMBS community that we can reach with a post or a message. Even if 3-4 of these people actually read the discussion posts and respond, that is 3-4 more people that we reached.

Find your voice, and remember:

Sales Tenet #4: Speak human.

4 - The Sales Process: Prospecting & New Calls

Sales Tenet #5: A lead is only a person of interest. A prospect is a qualified individual for whom your product or service is a clear match.

Cold Calls vs. New Calls

By definition, a cold call is an outbound sales call to someone with whom you've never spoken, nor do you know if that person has heard of or is aware of your company or service. In business selling, you must make outbound calls to people you don't know, but not cold calls.

Making a cold call means grabbing a phone book or a purchasing a lead list from an outside vendor, starting with the As and working through the Zs. This is telemarketing, not selling, and this type of cold calling is a complete waste of time. Never, ever cold call. If your business relies on cold calls, stop reading this book or find a new business.

Instead, you need to make "new calls." A new call begins by identifying and targeting individuals through research on company websites, LinkedIn, or conference attendee lists, and then delivering a customized message based on assessed need and product solutions. They are "new calls" because you are establishing a new connection with a new person. They are not cold calls, because you should know a considerable amount of information about the person you are calling first. More so, the person you are calling expects you to know a significant amount of information about them before you call.

Prospecting

If you prospect correctly and circulate in the places where your target customers circulate, you will never, ever have to make a traditional cold call.

Prospecting means that you are:

1. Calling qualified individuals that are engaged with your drip marketing (opening reports, for example), have registered on your website, and read your blog via RSS.

2. Calling people that are not doing any of these and don't know that you or your company exist, but are clearly individuals that can and should use your product.

Image by Tony Oliver from Denver, CO, USA (Prospector) [CC-BY-2.0 (http://creativecommons.org/licenses/by/2.0)], via Wikimedia Commons http://commons.wikimedia.org/wiki/File:Gold_prospector.jpg

Despite what it sounds like, this is not cold-calling.

For our company, we receive 15-20 registrations per day on our website. Every qualified person receives a phone call from us. Why do I use the term "qualified person"? Because not every person that falls into #1 above is qualified. For example, if you're selling enterprise software targeted at law firms and a real estate broker registers on your website, you need not call that person unless you have lots of spare time (which you shouldn't have). Someday down the road, after you've developed your business in your industry vertical, then by all means call that person to discover if there are applications for your product in another industry. Right now, you need to stay focused on your target.

Now, back to your qualified individuals... Some of these leads will become prospects. They profusely thank you for calling when they answer, ask questions about your product or service, are clearly interested, and happily engage in the sales process with you.

For many others, you'll land in voicemail and usually you won't get a return call. You can up your percentage significantly with some effort. (See Chapter 2 – "Pick up the Phone".) When you reach out and make these phone calls, you are prospecting.

In making these calls, you will find early adopters often because they found you. These early adopters may have started on Google searching a specific key word and found you, or they found your blog and company through Quora or Twitter. These people are gold and establishing the right path to convert them from Leads to Prospects quickly is critical to building your sales process and customer base.

When you are prospecting, you will be calling people you've never talked to before; these are "new calls." Those people have never heard of you or your company, and many times they don't know that they have the problem that you're going to solve for them. When you pick up the phone and call them, it's still not a cold call, as long as you are prospecting correctly. You cannot rely on single conference, event, speaking opportunity, press release, news article, deal, or announcement for sales growth. Sales growth stems from a clear sales process that begins with sound prospecting.

Outbound Calling & Prospecting

Let's say you:

1. Blog regularly about your industry
2. Sent out a few press releases and free reports
3. Stay active on Twitter and LinkedIn
4. Drip to email addresses you've acquired from your conference and industry research
5. Receive coverage in TechCrunch

Yet, the phone isn't ringing with people ready to buy your product. This is normal and this is why you have to prospect. You need to go out and find people, and most importantly, generate interest by identifying an individual's business problem and showing how your product solves that problem.

Now, if you're busy and you have a pipeline of solid sales opportunities from establishing and sharing your voice, by all means, skip the outbound calling. However, if you're still not getting the traction and inbound leads you need, you will need to sit down, buckle up, and start calling people you don't know. Here's how you do it:

Establish Call Blocks

These are 3-4 hour blocks of time when you are engaged in targeted calling activities. I suggest call blocks for a few reasons:

Reason #1: It's exhausting

If you're prospecting and doing it correctly - doing the research before the call, presenting ideas to customers during the call, and establishing specific takeaways for both sides to complete - you should, and will, get tired. This is a mentally taxing exercise. After 3-4 hours, you'll start slipping, because you'll forget if you've explained something already to the person you're calling, and most of all, you will lose enthusiasm and effectiveness as your energy decreases.

As soon as you notice this, take a break. Go for a walk outside around the block in the sun or the rain to force your body to change its physical demeanor. Think about your calls and debrief with yourself. Get frustrated. It means you care and you're stretching your domain to new customers.

When you get back to your desk, write down notes from your personal debriefing and start again for another 1-2 hours. If you've done your prospecting calls the right way, after 3-4 hours of calling, you should have made 10-15 calls with 2-3 specific future calls established for later in the week.

Reason #2: You can shut off your email for a couple of hours.

You need to focus on the person you are calling. This is impossible if you are staring at your email and a new message comes in the queue from another prospect that is returning your correspondence. You will instantly become distracted.

Everything else can wait, emails from marketing, engineering, and even your board members. If they complain about not getting back to them right away, tell him you were growing the company's revenue. If they still complain, stop working with that person. (Heck, even just now as I was editing this section, I jumped over to Twitter for just a second and almost clicked on the headline about Yahoo! announcing its new CEO!) If a customer emails you and says, 'EMAIL ME RIGHT AWAY!' then you haven't trained them properly to use customer service.

Turn it off.

Reason #3: Master your schedule.

It becomes predictable for everyone else around you in the company. Your developers and employees will learn not to bother you when you're in a call block. You become master of your schedule.

Tips for Successful Time Blocks

1. Have your call list prepared and printed in hard copy. This will give a targeted list, so you aren't wasting time digging around in your CRM for the contact info of people you want to call next. Plus there is a 95% probability that you'll get distracted while in your CRM with something else - another lead comes in, you realized you hadn't called so-and-so in a month, you see that you forgot to include the URL of an account in their profile and decide to take two seconds to do that. These are all unnecessary distractions.

2. Use sticky notes, so that you can see your progress. Develop a color coding system if you need to, green for calls that lead to a successful conversation, yellow for a contact made but without a significant or successful conversation, and blue for voicemails. Post these on your wall or window so that you can see your progress during the time block. When you're done, use the sticky notes as a check list of follow-up requirements for yourself. Whatever your chose, develop some sort of system that enables you to see the results of your daily work.

3. Set up a reward system for yourself. Once you hit 20 calls, reward yourself with 5 more calls after you get back from your walk. Then, buy a deluxe coffee instead of your regular small drip for making your 20 calls. I bring my workout clothes and go to the gym or on a run after a call block. You should be too mentally tired to do anything terribly cerebral, so this is a great time to re-energize for the rest of the day and feel good about yourself. Make a pact with your development team or office mates. Tell them that if you make 20 calls that include 10 contacts and 3 demos scheduled for later in the week, you'll take them to lunch. Believe me, whether your office mates work with you or not, they'll be pestering you to do more calls. Everyone likes a free lunch, even if it's a burrito from the local shop. Even better, you can make it a working lunch and go with a purpose and a topic to discuss.

Record your calls

You must (yes, must) dedicate time to learn how to refine and deliver your pitch quickly. Our sales team records calls regularly, and we critique them, looking specifically for three aspects of the call that went well and three opportunities to improve.

There are many services, such as Vonage and Onebox, that offer call recording options. Use them. It will be horrifying to listen to your voice and then count the "ums" and "ahs", but it is the only way to improve your call quality. What to look for as you review your calls:

- Listen for your delivery, your confidence, and your enthusiasm.

- Count the number of sentences you speak in a row before the customer has a chance to speak.

- Count the number of interruptions or talk-overs in your call. Are you talking over the customer or finishing their question before they have a chance to finish it? Are they talking over you because you don't understand their questions?

- Chart the total number of sentences you say compared to the customer. You have two ears and one mouth; you should be listening twice as much as you are talking. Sales calls must be interactive to be successful. You're not pitching for a time-share in Boca Raton – you're solving business problems and this requires collaboration.

Call Targeting & Counts

So how many calls should you make in a day? The short answer is, "it depends." It depends on:

1. Who you're calling, i.e., C-level execs with gatekeepers with skilled receptionists or senior/mid-level managers.

2. Why you're calling, i.e., "Dialing for dollars" versus calling to establish a business relationship. If you are "dialing for dollars," that's telemarketing and doesn't apply to what we're discussing in this book.

Here are few personal examples that assume you are calling to introduce yourself and establish a business relationship, with the objective to initiate a longer term sales process that might take weeks, months, or even years to close.

Software Product: Higher Education Market

Call Target: University professors

Calls: 15-25/day

Call Objective: Establish relationship, set up product demo call for the next week. Sales goal is for adoption of online software for use in the following semester's courses, a 3-6 month sales process.

Process: Because most professors have a department-supplied webpage and an online vita, there's a huge amount of information available about them, including classes taught, syllabi, research interest, office hours, and personal educational background. It was easy to see their teaching styles (lecture vs. discussion vs. experimental), assignments from their syllabi, and their research interest. This information made it simple to develop a questioning strategy for the initial call. As I reviewed each professor in the department, I delineated between those professors which appeared to be a more qualified prospect than others, such as taught the classes that matched our software content, took an experimental teaching approach, and taught the same courses frequently.

Call preparation: Took 5-15 minutes to read the online info available and write out a call guide, questions I planned to ask and how I expected to lead the conversation. Separately, there was the voicemail script should I receive a voicemail (common in academia) but when you get them on the phone, they can be a chatty bunch. (Professors are teachers and they have less allegiance to a regular schedule, so if I asked the right questions, an initial call could easily go 30-45 minutes.)

Finally, I personalized a follow up email, which was another 5-10 minutes per call.

An average day would be 15-20 calls. A big day would be 25-30, but this also meant fewer connections. It was far better to make 15 calls and have 4-5 substantial conversations than make 30 calls with 29 voicemails.

Each substantial conversation usually entailed setting up a custom sample course for the professor to view, and then scheduling a 30-60 minute demo call within the next few days. This meant that after a few days of effective prospecting, my next few days would be full with demos. From 20 initial calls, I usually scheduled 2-3 demos for a few days ahead. Completing four demos in a day was full day with preparation, set-up, pump-up, and follow-up afterwards. I might do 20 prospecting calls a day for 2-3 days, and then not do any for several days.

Analytics & Data: Financial Market Trading Desks & Investment Funds

Call Target: C-level executives, Managing Directors, Traders, Fund Managers

Calls: 15-25/day

Call Objective: Establish relationship, learn investment positions and fund size, ask "Situational" questions, and set up an initial product demo call for the next week.

Process: Most targets have LinkedIn profiles, so I spend about 15 minutes prior to each call researching the person's background and their fund, and preparing questions and an effective voicemail script.

Generally, the same outcome is sought as in the first example, generate interest through Situational questions, and then set up a more substantive call for a few days or a week later to look at sample data and research together.

Commercial Real Estate: Community Banks, Regional Banks, Credit Unions

Call Target: Senior VP of Operations, Operations Managers

Calls: 20 calls in 4 hours; 40-50 for the day.

Call Objective: Establish relationship, set up face-to-face meetings with our broker.

Process: This was pre-LinkedIn (2003), but banks already posted their senior management bios, so that was a start. Then, I would research that bank in places like Business Journal for articles about mergers, buyouts, or new branch expansion. This would enable me to speak intelligently about their real estate and location needs.

A Sales Management Note about Inside Sales

Do not mistake "inside sales" with "telesales." Telesales are useful for the $50/month product or satellite TV. A true inside sales professional is a highly skilled individual who is able to develop relationships, read customer psychology, generate interaction effectively on a product demonstration, and motivate the prospect to take action - all over the phone.

If you're selling at the enterprise level, the initial point of contact is as critical as the initial sales presentation and approving the final contract. Who would you rather have talking with a conference lead or a Senior VP that just downloaded a white paper on your company's website, a technical inside sales professional or an inexperienced telesales person?

Onsite Visits

Enterprise-level sales and technology are complex. You may get to a point when you will go onsite to meet with a prospect. However, that will only be after you have developed a sound fundamental relationship with a clear path in the sales process. Everyone is too busy to host you onsite even if you've flown 2000 miles for an initial conversation about your product or service. There are months of preparation to invest in the sales process before you earn the right to do an onsite visit. Yes, get personal and break down the walls, but only go onsite when you have a really, really good reason. And, it will usually take an incredible amount of phone work before you have that reason. For several of my biggest customers, I have never met them in person or visited them onsite

No one likes meetings. We try to use phrases like, "How about I swing by the office?" or "I'll be downtown this afternoon - I'll stop by." Sure, it sounds easy, but fact is that your clients are busy. That 10 am "pop by" meeting means they have to block an hour from their day for the meeting, plus they lose the 30 minutes before the meeting in which they can't dive into anything substantial because you'll be arriving soon. If your contact is a manager, the 30 minutes after the meeting are blown. Everyone needs to talk to him just after your meeting, because he's been unavailable for the last hour. Then, it's almost lunch so he can't dive into anything substantial right away, not to mention that he may also want to wear a slightly nicer shirt that day because he doesn't want you to get the wrong impression, which means he has to remember to pick up the dry cleaning or ask his wife to do it. Then, she forgets and they have an argument - all because you wanted to "pop by" the office. Yes, a little sarcasm here, but you get the point.

Enterprise and senior managers are notorious for resisting meetings and "pop-bys." In the capital markets industry, these guys live in front on their Bloomberg terminals. When we do visit the big banks and funds, it's usually downstairs in the common area or first floor conference room, because they don't want you interrupting their workplace. So, if you are invading their space, you better make it good. Do something that you otherwise could not have accomplished over the phone. That might be reviewing a complex topic or examining an intricate detail of your product and how it relates to a core problem the prospect has.

Reminder: PICK UP THE PHONE

The phone is your umbilical cord to the market. The market and your buyers know this. Because of that, if you are skilled and professional on the phone, you will be able to progress a sale just as well over the phone as you would in person, if not better.

At Prudential CRES, every broker every day sat in their cubicle and made phone calls, even though they were selling real estate right there in San Francisco. They were not visiting clients all day every day; the opportunity costs are too high. You can get an enormous amount of work and selling accomplished over the phone, if you do it effectively.

The market also knows that the phone is their shield from you. Everyone expects that no one expects them to call a salesperson back when they receive a voicemail. This means you must be skilled at connecting and establishing value with your prospects. You must also be resilient to these expectations and be repetitive in your outreach through multiple channels, phone, personal emails, blog, and newsletters, anything that gives you a reason to call your prospects. You need to give them a reason to take your calls, return your calls, or spend five minutes with you when they do answer the phone.

Remember:

Sales Tenet #5: A lead is only a person of interest. A prospect is a qualified individual for whom your product or service is a clear match.

5 - Prospecting at Conferences

Conferences are daunting and expensive, and they are a complete waste of time, unless you are exceptionally prepared. As you are ramping up your business and sales pipeline, go to the events and avoid registration fees at all costs. There is plenty of LobbyCon you can do. It will be painfully obvious when it's time to actually pay to register. Don't feel bad about this.

Aerial view of the crowd in an exhibition hall at computer trade show CeBIT in 2000.
http://commons.wikimedia.org/wiki/File:CeBIT_2000_exhibition_hall.jpg

To Booth or Not to Booth

If you're not sure whether you should plunk down the cash for a booth, then you shouldn't. You'll know when it's time. Booths do provide a nice meeting place and you will get a few quality leads, if you have a clear booth strategy. However, consider the hard and opportunity costs of a booth as a small company or worse, if you're by yourself. Consider this – booth traffic comes in waves between sessions or during lunch and coffee breaks. You might get a swarm of people for an hour, and then nothing for a couple of hours. If you are a one-man show, you can only talk to one person at a time. What do you do when you have three people standing aside poking their head over the shoulder of the guy to whom you're demoing your product, and whom you know isn't a good fit based on your short conversation? Professional courtesy dictates that you be nice and continue the demo with him. Meanwhile, you are distracted, wondering if the three people that looked interested but walked away were possibly your next great customer. It's a tough racket. Think about it before you spend $10,000 on the booth.

Generating Appointments

Yes, you should go to conferences, but not because you want to stand at a booth for three days. You should be setting up appointments based on the attendee list and people that are reading your outbound drip emails and newsletters (Constant Contact is an excellent tool for tracking email open rates: www.constantcontact.com). If you can't book at least 4-5 appointments per day of the conference, then you either need to try harder or stay home. It's a losing gamble to show up to a conference without a book of appointments expecting that you will randomly bump into a brand new qualified prospect that is ready to buy your product in the next three months. That's hope and desperation, not reality.

If it's a three-day conference, compress your meetings into two days. Go back-to-back-to-back to optimize your time and save a few dollars on one fewer hotel night. Besides, compressing your schedule into two days also forces you to be efficient with your time.

Look for registration names at industry conferences and events. At a minimum, the event organizers post the company names attending. You can call into the main number of these companies and ask for the department that is most relevant to your product. From there, ask which people from the company are attending the conference. Whoever you talk to will either know immediately ("Oh that's probably Michelle; she's our Managing Director and attends all of these conferences.") or can transfer you to the department admin that will know.

Use your email list and blog to announce that you're going and set up a date book. Here's a template that I've used. It is admittedly passive, but gives a specific reason for the recipient to respond. There's a fine line between too passive and too aggressive. Play around with your market and contacts to see what works best for you.

Subject: Going to the ABSEast in Miami next week?

Just a quick note to see if you're attending the ABSEast conference in Miami next week. I'll be there with our Market Analytics team (booth #122) to walk through our new Forward Valuation Model launched this month.

If you are, shoot me a quick reply so we can get together - booth, coffee, meeting before/after sessions - whatever works.

Many thanks - looking forward to your reply.

-Scott

This type of email is an excellent start to setting up a dance card for yourself, starting a month before the conference. In this case, I had the luxury of a booth because we had a team of people attending. If you aren't setting up a booth, try something like this:

Subject: Going to the ABSEast in Miami next week?

Just a quick note to see if you're attending the ABSEast conference in Miami next week. I'll be there and wanted to schedule a few minutes with you. My team released our new Forward Valuation Model this month and I thought you'd be a great person for a few perspectives on it. I'll treat to a real Starbucks, not the fake kind they say they brew by the gallon and give away for free at the conference.

Just reply back with a time or two that works with your schedule.

Many thanks - looking forward to your reply.

-Scott

The really busy executives and decision-makers that you want to meet often have event planners that keep a master schedule. The biggest companies will have their own meeting rooms and their dance cards fill up very quickly – they have customers too. They prefer selling over buying while they're at the conference. This is why you need develop a relationship early and often by adding value and integrating yourself into their work practice. Start at least two months ahead of a big conference, if you want to make it on the dance card of these big companies.

Here's an example from a large company that's a lot of fluff. There's no way anyone is reading this email. This email requires me to enable my view of images in my email and scroll to read the entire message. Sending the email to "undisclosed participants" is a nice personal touch too… Jeez…

You're a small company – be personal. Speak human. (See Chapter 3 – "Find Your Voice".)

Tactical Tips

<u>Look for registration names at industry conferences and events.</u> If nothing else, these events post the company names attending. You can call into the main number of these companies and ask for the department that is most relevant to your product. Go to the events, but avoid registration fees at all costs. There is plenty of "LobbyCon" you can do. It will be painfully obvious when it's time to actually pay to register. Don't feel bad about this. Yes, I am purposely repeating these points.

<u>Get to know the companies and people running the events and always submit for speaking slots.</u> You'd be amazed how many times the conference organizers have speaker and panel needs, experience cancellations, and are searching for new perspectives on stale industry topics. This is a good way to get free registrations and showcase your expertise. But, also know that

the big conferences usually save speaking spots for sponsors and supporters. That's just the way it is.

Offer to volunteer. See if the conference organizers need volunteers to help for a few hours with checking badges, chair drops, or pointing attendees to the correct sessions. A couple of hours might yield you a free pass and lots of good will.

Ride the escalator. You never know who you're going to meet plus you can read nametags of people going in the opposite direction. You'll have a fixed audience in an open setting versus the fictitious "elevator pitch." Elevators are uncomfortably quiet and everyone departs at different floors. On an escalator, everyone is going to the same place, the next floor. Then, you can get off at any floor with the person you've met and walk with them to the next session. It's open aired and thus less psychologically restricting for conversation.

Get an iPad. It reduces the psychological wall introduced by laptop clamshells and speeds up the "let me show it to you" transition for your one-on-one meetings.

Condense your demo to five (5) minutes and then ask questions. You are not selling (in the traditional sense) at the conference. Your job is to pique interest and get an advance in the sales process. It's unlikely the person you're meeting can decide "yea" or "nay" on your product right then, right away. Instead, have a quick five (or three) minute demo ready. Then, be armed with questions specific to the prospect and a suggested path to continue the sales conversation after you both return to your respective offices. This must be specific. Specific is not when your prospect says, "Looks good – give me a call in a week or so after the dust settles." Specific is when your prospect says, "This looks interesting. Let's have a call with John Smith who runs our software management group. He's usually best to grab early in the week. Send him an email and copy me on it to arrange a demo next week."

Ask: "What brings you to the conference?" (Attribution to Mike Simonsen www.linkedin.com/in/simonsen) This gives you the core reason to address in your conversation and tie your product to the over-arching strategy or problem the prospect has on their mind. Some people go for a set of specific presentations. Some people are speakers. Some people go because their manager made them. In any of these situations, you've opened a conversation channel to learn more about that person and if your product will help them. Read industry publications and ask your prospect for their opinion about conference topics. You'll be surprised how this type of conversation unveils true customer sentiments and ultimately their product needs.

Set goals for yourself for small time blocks. For example, "Have three substantial conversations with potential leads at the opening breakfast" or "exchange business cards with at least five speakers from the afternoon sessions." This will keep you motivated and focused at the task at hand, developing relationships and finding new prospects.

Blog about a session you attended. Take notes in a couple of sessions and type up a blog post summarizing a few key statements. Provide a paragraph of your own perspective and commentary on the topic. You can also use your article post-conference to talk with people that didn't attend. Now, you're adding real value (See Chapter 7 – "Build with Value"). I did this at an event and posted to my Seeking Alpha blog. The conference organizers saw it and asked if they could re-post it on the conference website. Um… yes! See: _http://seekingalpha.com/article/126728-rmbs-opportunities-in-2009-recap-from-imn-s-distressed-investment-summit_

At the Conference

Conferences are for advances. If you can't get a meeting with a prospect, they're not a prospect yet. It means that you haven't yet illustrated enough value to them. As you are developing your schedule prior to the conference, you will receive a few – "Just call me when you get there and we'll find a time." You definitely should do exactly that, but don't depend on these appointments to fill your day.

If the prospect keeps the meeting you scheduled, you better be darn ready to advance the relationship. No one wants to meet for coffee or chat. Everyone at the conference is spending time away from the office and their families while getting further behind every hour that passes. If they are at the conference, they want to learn new information that they otherwise would not have discovered. Give them some excitement and inspiration that their really hard problem at work can be solved with your product. If they are at the conference because they have to be, then be their inspiration; make them happy their boss made them go.

If you set up a booth, have a system. A real system. Putting business cards in a box is not a system. Writing notes on the back of cards is not a system. A system is having a tear sheet with the top 10 questions you would like to ask each booth visitor. It should be easy to fill out. Have a stapler to attach the business card to the question sheet. Use it like an order pad as you are talking with them and fill it out with them. I prefer hand written notes over an iPad or electronic scanner, because it is more personal to the prospect. This shows your visitors that you are interested in understanding their business and discovering their Critical Business Issue. Call it that. If they ask, tell them that unless they have a problem equivalent to their house on fire and you are the fire department, insurance company, and grief counselor combined, you both know that you won't be doing business together, because that's how things work. This conveys your seriousness and they will respect you for it.

<u>People will blow you off</u>. If a prospect tells you "I'll stop by the booth," about one out of five actually will, and then you know you have a good prospect. The rest are blowing you off because you haven't displayed enough value to them yet or they missed you during that one time you ran to the bathroom.

<u>If you book a meeting and they cancel or don't show, be nice, try again, then move on and put them back into your drip marketing pile</u>. It means you haven't shown them enough value. I was introduced to a very good prospect (or so I thought) about a month before a very big industry conference. He agreed to a meeting at the conference based on our preliminary phone conversations. He then proceeded to delay our 11:00 am meeting to 12:30 pm, and then to 1:30pm by texting that he was late "because I wanted to get in a workout." When he showed at the booth, he spent half of the time checking his Blackberry instead of engaging in the conversation. When he came up for air, he completely dismissed our product approach and said it would not work for him. That was it. Six months later at another industry conference, we agreed to another meeting, which he cancelled about an hour before we were scheduled. Guess what? He is not a prospect.

<u>People that hang out at your booth for long periods of time usually don't have anything else to do and probably aren't going to be customers</u>. It means they probably like you personally and they think they're doing you a favor by keeping you busy. All they are really doing is wasting your time, because they have time to waste and aren't interested in getting busier, making decisions about your product, or building their own business (in which case they won't be very good customers anyway). Be nice, excuse yourself and go walk the conference floor to find new people to meet.

<u>Bring Starbucks Via, Altoids, Power Bars, a big bag of raw nuts, and Purell</u>. Conference coffee is awful; it's watery and never has enough caffeine to do the trick for me. Fill your coffee cup and lace it with Starbucks Via. The Altoids keep your mind and mouth fresh from drinking coffee. Power Bars are adequate replacements for missed meals. Nuts are a filling alternative to the sugary cookies and Nutri-Grain bars served during breaks. Purell keeps you germ free. Not everyone washes their hands.

<u>Never eat in your booth</u>. It's unprofessional and is deters would be visitors to your booth, because most people are nice and they don't want to interrupt you while you're eating.

Eating & Prospecting

<u>Eat small portions of food so you can stick and move</u>. Take small portions at the breakfast, lunches, and happy hour buffets, so you can circulate quickly. The meals are usually served buffet style and attendees are left to find a place to stand or sit and eat. There are usually too few places with just a few standing bar top tables. By taking small portions, you can belly up to a table or group, have a round of conversations, find out if any are potential leads, exchange cards, and move on with, "Wow those egg rolls are really good. I'm going to grab another one. It's been really nice chatting with you. I'll call you next Tuesday when you're back in your office."

<u>Drink club soda</u>. Alcohol makes you stupid. You're there to build your business, not drink free Bud Light. Avoid tonic water. It has a lot of sugar in it.

<u>Take an etiquette class</u>. How do you eat unpitted olives served in your salad? How do you hold a conversation in a 10-person round table format? Where does your fork and knife go after you've finished? Trust me. Spend $100 on a really good etiquette class and learn these things. It matters.

<u>Learn to say "Let's swap."</u> As a conversation wraps up, potential prospects will often say to you, "Give me your card and I'll give you a call next week." They won't call, not because they're jerks, but because they're busy and forget. When they ask for your card, say, "Sure thing. Let's swap." This gives you control and permission to contact them. If they say, "Oh jeez, I ran out" or "I left them in my room," then say, "No problem!" Pull out your notebook and pen (See Chapter 1 – "Handling Inbound Calls & Leads"), flip to a clean page and say, "Just write down your info here." You will look professional and prepared. Review what they wrote to make sure you have their spelling and contact information correct.

Final Thoughts

- When you're at the conference, send reminders and confirmations for all of your meetings. You will get cancellations in reply to your confirmation message. That's okay. It tells you that either that person isn't a good meeting or you did a poor job showing the value of getting together. Sometimes, the person decided not to travel after all for personal reasons and will ask you to call them after the conference.

- If you use text messaging for confirming, then begin every text with, "Hi [prospect name], [your name] from [your company]." It makes the text more personal and it's likely that your prospect won't recognize your cell phone number. Treat it like a mini-email.

Spelling counts. End with a question to confirm receipt and acceptance. Take the extra time to do this. It makes a difference to your prospect. For example:

> *"Hi Ron, Scott from Altos. Confirming for our 10 am. Would you still like to meet at conference registration desk on the 2nd floor?"*

- Pick a central place to meet that is easy to find and close to everything else, such as the conference registration desk, not the hotel registration desk. It's too busy and usually too far from the conference activity.

- You can always walk to the coffee shop or lobby together. Use the walk and store line to exchange niceties, so you can transition to business talk when you grab a table. If you meet at the coffee shop, that time goes ephemeral. When you get to the coffee shop, order an Odwalla or sparkling water. You've probably already had too much coffee anyway and the fresh juice or water will do you good.

Assume that 1/4 to 1/3 of your appointments will either bail on you or be a no-show. Don't take this personally. It's just the way it is. Use the missed connection as a reason to set up a call the week after the conference. Just like your onsite meetings, you absolutely, positively must give the other person a clear reason why they should meet with you.

6 - More Sales Process

Sales Tenet #6: A prospect's decision criteria is a formative process. It will always take more than a single phone call to determine.

Sales Tenet #7: It's never about the money; it's about the cost.

Chapter 4, "The Sales Process - Prospecting & New Calls", and Chapter 5, "Prospecting at Conferences", focused on the prospecting area of the sales process, differentiating between leads and prospects and how to develop prospects using a clear set of techniques. These techniques will bring you to the start the sales process. Let me repeat that – *these techniques will bring you the start of the sale process*. Until now, you are simply qualifying leads and vetting prospects. In some of these conversations, your leads and prospects will tell you, "Wow! This is exactly what we need!" Don't call your partners and investors to tell them you closed a deal. What did you do? You *opened* a sale and *started* the sales process with this company. The next stages include multiple product demonstrations, working through committees, developing decision criteria, and finding out who holds the purse strings. This can take weeks, and more likely, months to accomplish.

Now, we'll examine the questions to ask that will firmly entrench yourself into the sales process with your target prospect. It's a grind, and if you know what to expect and what's happening while it's happening, you'll be in control of the grind. Starting the sales process is a challenge itself. Once you're in the process, achieving advances in this stage are possible only through effective questioning that shows your prospect that you are both keenly aware of and interested in solving their problem.

Example: Did I just Open or Close a Sale?

Last year, I spent a solid ten months developing a very large prospect. This included several calls to my main point of contact who recently joined this account from other firm where I first met and worked with him. He arranged an onsite meeting with his peers, though he was personally unable to attend. We met in person at a conference that year and I logged more than 30 phone calls to him and his co-workers concurrently with our regular drip marketing throughout the year. He articulated a clear need for our data products and saw several places to implement these throughout their organization.

This contact then organized a sales demonstration to the key decision-makers in the company and we were off to the races. We hosted the demonstration on GoToMeeting and all of the key players attended. They asked specific questions and I could hear them envisioning the use of our products. As the demonstration call wound down, the action item was left for our main contact to coordinate the feedback from the attendees and then he and I would discuss next steps on their decision. Immediately after the call, our Product Champion and I did a quick review. He said that the call was EXACTLY what the team needed to see and that it articulated the need for our products. Woohoo!

About two weeks passed and after several outbound calls and voicemail, I finally was able to connect with our contact on the phone for a short conversation. He was clearly busy, but willing to offer an update on their business. They have been extremely busy buying assets and setting up a new investment fund. Growth is good. We turned the conversation to the demonstration call.

He said that the right people were in the room to see what they should be buying and they bought into the concept. This is the right point to get them thinking about these types of products. He said that they decided now that they "most definitely will subscribe to market data whether that be from your company or someone else" and that he would give me an update at the end of the week or early next.

Here's the point: **All of that groundwork got us to the starting gate of the sale. We've established a need, but have only started the sales process without any real analysis begun from the senior managers at the fund as to how they might implement our products to solve the problem they have now articulated for themselves.**

Questions & the Complexity of the Sale

The objective in the early stage of the sales process is asking effective, intelligent questions that enable you and your prospect to determine that a need exists, and that your product or services can potentially fill that need.

The complexity of the enterprise sale is very real and cannot be circumvented. If you have an "in" with a big company, be optimistic and be cautious. If this person tells you, "I love your product. Send me all of your materials and I'll present it to the team" then your contact is not a decision-maker and you are only at the start of the process. If your "in" is a senior level executive, remember that really good managers attain buy-in from their downstream team.

Few managers will make a singular decision to implement a new product or service without checking with the team, because the team will be the ones implementing and using the new product. Additionally, junior managers may already have discovered other outside vendors. Internally, the team could be developing an in-house solution that will not only be 100% customized, but provide job security to those working on the project.

10 Questions You Should Ask On Every Sales Call

Relax. It's a conversation, not an interrogation. Have courage; you're allowed to ask questions. It's daunting at first, because you want to placate the prospect. They are sitting there on their "Throne of Decision-Maker" and you are visualizing dollar signs all around their head, knowing that closing a deal this size means you can hire another developer or begin renting office space.

Here are ten questions to ask that will turn your sales interrogations into sales conversations:

1. <u>How do you mean?</u> (Attribution to Brian Tracy, "The Psychology of Selling") Prospects will tell you all kinds of things on a call. Much of it won't make sense. Ask this question to clarify what they're thinking, so you can be 100% sure you understand what they're communicating.

1b. <u>I don't think I understood – would you mind running that by me one more time?</u> This is a variation of "How do you mean?" You're allowed to ask for clarification. The prospect is a prospect, not the great and powerful Oz. Take a moment to ask for another run-through of what they've just explained. It is probably complicated and they probably know it. They'll appreciate that you want to comprehend their problem fully so that you prescribe a treatment for it with your incredibly awesome product.

2. <u>What's the most important part of your business?</u> The idea here is to dig to the root of the prospect's existence, so you can eventually unearth the critical business issue on which you're going to sell your product. Be careful! You must be truly interested in the answer to this question and give the prospect a reason for asking. More so, this can't be a question that can be answered on the prospect's company website. Also, I don't recommend asking this question as your first question, because it can sound trite and patronizing. Instead, ask specific process and problem questions first and, after developing rapport, circle back to this question. A good transition is something like – "Okay, so I think I understand your process pretty well, though I'm sure I'll have more questions. Let me ask you this – what's the most important part of your business?" This is a much smoother transition to this question and your prospect will be more apt to answer truthfully now that he's confided in you about his current process and problems.

3. <u>How would this help your business?</u> This question gets the customer doing two things: 1) It gets the prospect envisioning the use of your product, and 2) It gives you the selling points to drive at the rest of the conversation.

4. <u>Why is that important? How important is that?</u> Prospects like to push, just to see what you have, and usually they don't know they're pushing. Or, they're just naturally inquisitive. Here's an example:

Prospect: "Is your platform built in Java?"

Now, what if your platform is built in Ruby or Python? The customer is asking a simple question that you can easily interpret as, "Oh, my gosh, the customer said it has to be in Java! We're doomed! What do I do? Do I tell them it's not, but that we're willing to replicate the entire code base in Java for him if that's what he needs?"

You: Instead of freaking out or answering, "No, we built our platform in Ruby," answer with, "It's not – why do you ask?" (a variation of "why is that important?"). Here are a number of responses you might hear to your well-formed question:

- "Oh just curious. Seems that a lot of software platforms are built in Java."

- "Thank God, I'm a huge fan of Ruby."

- "I dunno. I'm not much of a programmer myself, so I just thought I should ask that question."

- "Hmmm… We prefer software built in Java, but we can work with any tool." You ask, "Why is that?" and you're on your way to understanding and defining part of the decision criteria.

Notice how none of these four responses above are showstoppers for you, but had you simply replied with, "No, it's built in Ruby", you never would have discovered this path. Remember, your sales calls are conversations, not interrogations.

Don't panic; just ask them how important the particular feature is to their work. Usually, it's not very important. For those times it is important, you'll be able to build that functionality into your product later. If you can't, then chances are the competition can't either.

5. <u>What are the 2-3 most important objectives for your business this year/this quarter?</u> This question will drive right to those areas that the prospect most cares about each and every day. If they tell you, "Well, senior management is really focusing on growing our revenue with the blah-blah product line. We spent a lot of money developing and marketing the product and they want to see results." Bingo. Determine how your product or service will get them there. This hits home personally too. Your prospect is a normal guy. Maybe he has a wife and a third child on the way and he needs to buy a better car or a bigger house? Maybe he wants to get out of his two bedroom apartment and move to the suburbs, where the schools are better. Help him get there. By asking him this question, you become a member of his personal team achieving his professional objectives.

6. <u>Why haven't you purchased the product yet?</u> This question is more for an opportunity that is losing momentum. If you ask directly, you should get a direct answer like, "It's just that our IT team is so backed up with other projects, I can't add this to their

plate right now" or "We've have a stop on all new purchases until we get into next year." Okay, now you have your objections to overcome. If it is the former, figure out how you can assist with implementation. Fly there and install it yourself. If it is the second, do a delay billing until next year. If they resist either of these, then you haven't found the real reason they aren't buying yet or you haven't identified their critical business issue and how your product solves it.

7. <u>"Here's why I'm asking. We've had our development team locked in a dark smoky room for the last six months, working on several new product initiatives, and I think that several of them will help you guys [make more money/win more bids/etc.]. My team and I have a fixed amount of time to spend with our customers, so the reason for asking is so that we can decide if there's a real opportunity to work together."</u> This is a follow up to #6 if you think the answer you received was a bland "time" or "budget" excuse. This is also the takeaway close and it's selling without showing or talking product. If they tell you, "That's okay. Just come back to us in Q1 of next year", then move them back to your marketing drip, set a reminder to call the prospect in a month for a non-sales reason, and move along.

8. <u>"What's changed recently, or do you see changing in your business in the next 3, 6, 12 months?"</u> Just listen. Don't sell or pitch products. Take notes, and come back to the client with specific ideas based on what you learned. Treat these meetings as you would an information-gathering sales call with a new lead or prospect. You wouldn't try to sell on the first call with a new prospect, so don't do it here.

An advantage to this approach is that if your customer has changes coming down the road, and you have a product in development or beta stage, it's an opportunity for you to get your product team involved with an existing customer as an early adopter or beta tester. The client benefits here because they are first to market, and you benefit because, assuming you have a solid relationship, if the new product fails in some way, there is less pressure on you and your company.

Additionally, you can also influence the strategic direction of your client by educating them on new products and services you have in development. Many times the client has an idea or a vision, but execution on that vision requires a product that doesn't exist. That presents an opportunity for you to define criteria for the purchase around the specs for your products in the development pipeline and blocking out your competition before an opportunity or "Request for Proposal" (RFP) becomes public.

9. <u>Who else on your team will you have evaluate the product?</u> If you ask, "Who else would be involved with making this decision?", then the prospect hears, "This guy doesn't think I'm important enough to make a decision on my own. And even though I'm not, that's so condescending." By framing the question in the suggested way instead, you are both feeding ego by showing that you expect the prospect to take the lead, while still finding out who is involved. Decisions are not made in a vacuum by a single person. Even if your prospect is the CEO of Home Depot, he is going to have his downstream team evaluate the product, because he knows that they know more about their business needs and how to implement solutions than he does. And, even if your prospect is the only person in the company that will be using the product on a day-to-day basis, the outcomes of his work will affect the team. Besides, if that prospect ever leaves the company, you're dead. Spread through the organization with as many contacts as possible early in the sales process. You will see a direct correlation between the number of contacts you have at a company and your sales. Places where you have 1-2 contacts are unlikely to become clients because it means either you have Gatekeepers or you are talking to the wrong people.

10. <u>What happens next?</u> (Attribution to Michael Pedone at SalesBuzz.com.) This establishes a specific course of action when the call ends. You need advances, not continuations. This gives you control by forcing them to set the next steps. They might say, "Well, I need to talk to Bob's group and tell them what I saw." Aha! Now, you've discovered there is another group involved with the decision, and you've uncovered a potential Gatekeeper. You can jump in and ask, "Tell me about Bob's group. How are they involved with your work?"

"Send me the presentation and your marketing materials and I'll share them with the rest of the group…"

If your sales calls end with this sentence, you're dead. Besides, I bet you don't have any marketing materials anyway. (This is another excellent reason why you should sparingly use PowerPoint slides in a presentation. It looks canned and your prospect thinks they are just another prospect watching a canned presentation.)

You absolutely, positively must push your way through this outcome and find a close. A "close" is simply an advance in the sales process. The perception of the salesperson winning the order with a slick presentation or closing line is completely fictitious. In fact, when you actually reach the contract stage of the sale, it will be anti-climactic (See Chapter 10 – "Negotiation & Contracts").

Think of closes as a compass to show you where you are with the prospect and the sales process. You need to find out what the next steps are going to be for both you and your prospects. This is why the "What happens next?" question is such a good one. If your prospect tells you, "Well, send me your marketing materials and I'll pass them here with the rest of the group", then you know you haven't shown enough value for your prospect to spend his internal capital rounding up his colleagues and plopping in a meeting to hear you talk. If your prospect says, "I'd like to have you present to the whole team next week", then you say, "Great, how about Tuesday afternoon at 2:00 pm?"

At first, asking for closes will inevitably feel clumsy. That's okay. Ask them anyway. By asking the right questions during the call, you should now know key aspects to the sale, the end users, the current problems and how you can solve them, and who else would be involved with the decision.

Here are a couple of suggested responses to the dreaded "Send me your materials" request:

- "You know what, I'd like to except that we really didn't look at any slides together. We were diving directly into the live application to show you how it works. Instead, let's do this: let's schedule a 20 minute time block next week with your team. Now that you've seen it and know how valuable it might be, I'm sure they're going to want to see it for themselves. I have my calendar open right now. How about on Tuesday at the same time?"

- "I can't let you torture yourself like that. I'm sure the people on your team will have a few questions and then you're stuck trying to remember every nuance that we covered today. Let's do this: let's schedule 20 minutes....[see above]."

- "Who are the other people on your team? I'll send the materials over to them and give them a call to answer their questions, that way you're now stuck being the middleman in the conversation. I'm sure you have enough to do every day, let alone worry about answering questions about our product."

If you are still meeting resistance, politely agree and say, "What day next week is best to give you call so we can discuss your team's feedback?" This forces them to agree to do the work to gather the feedback, or they will push back and say, "Well, I don't know if everyone will have time this week to look at the materials." Then, you can reply with, "Oh, okay. Let's do this then: let's hold off circulating the materials right now. I'll call you back next week to see if that's a better time to focus on this. I've got my calendar open right now. Is 1:00 on Monday okay to do that?"

If your prospect shares names, write them down and be sure to spell their names correctly. Then, personally call each one to let them know that you would like to talk with them directly. Do not blast one email to everyone on the list. Start working the committee that's now been formed. Treat every single person in the committee individually. Learn specific situations and needs. Before every call, spend time on Linkedin to develop targeted questions for each person.

Even More Sales Process

Just like with voicemails and phone strategies covered in Chapter 2 – "Pick up the Phone" – there more in-depth resources for immersing yourself into the excruciating details of the sales process and developing a new market for a new product. After finishing this book, read these two:

- "Major Account Sales Strategy" by Neil Rackham
- "Selling into a New Market Space" by Brian Burns

Concepts covered in these books that you must learn include:

- Product Champions: These are true believers in your product. They will cheerlead internally and help you navigate through their company's decision process.

- Continuations vs. Advances: You want advances. These are clear next steps that both sides agree to complete. For example, an advance is when your prospect agrees to send you a file for loading into your platform and sets an appointment for you to demonstrate to the team. A continuation means there is an unspecified next step, such as, "Call me next month and we'll set something up."

- Decision Committees: Decisions are not made in a vacuum. You need to know who are your protagonists, antagonists, end users, financiers, and contributors to the sales process.

- Phases of the Purchasing decision: If you are selling into an enterprise, the decision process will take several phone calls and interactions with the prospect. Know ahead of time that there are four major stages: Needs Analysis, Evaluation of Options, Resolution of Concerns, and Implementation. Within each stage, you will find a number of sub-stages. The sooner you become intimately knowledgeable with this process, the sooner you will be able to identify where each prospect stands in the sales process.

Remember:

Sales Tenet #6: The decision criteria is a formative process. It will always take more than a single phone call to determine.

Sales Tenet #7: It's never about the money; it's about the cost.

7 - Build with Value

Sales Tenet #8: Add value, add value, add value.

Add value, add value, add value. Your prospects are busy. Everyone is busy. When you ring the phone on their desk, you are interrupting something they are doing. That something might be a meeting (yes, people answer the phone while they are in a meeting), a conversation with a colleague, solving a really hard problem at work, wondering why their manager is in a bad mood, emailing with their kids about what time to pick them up from soccer practice, or anything else more important to them than you are at that moment. This means that when you make an outbound touch by phone or email, you absolutely positively must make it worthwhile for the prospect to stop whatever it is they are doing and pay attention to you.

Pitching a product five seconds into a phone call is not adding value. Spamming a list of people requesting a time to give them a call is not adding value. In our case, adding value is a very simple offering, our "National Housing Report." It's a monthly outbound touch that includes real-time data about the housing market, as of the most recent week. We send these reports to our contacts and track open rates. From these open rates, we now have a call list. If someone opens the report, that means we've provided value to them in some way. Otherwise, they would have ignored us. These contacts that open the reports are potential leads. Contacts that take our calls to talk about the data in the report are potential prospects. Contacts that return your calls and talk with you are definitely prospects.

You need to do all of this before you can justify a real opportunity with a prospect. When you add value, you earn the right to talk about your prospect's problems and how your product is their fix.

Valuable Content

- White Papers: White papers highlight your expertise and show your focus on solving your industry's business problems, and they are relatively inexpensive to produce because of the time involved. Take a few of your blog posts and expand them to three-page white papers. Then, convert them to PDF and post to your site. Have three or four of these. Writing the papers will crystallize many key challenges of your industry that you may be talking about without a truly informed perspective. Check out what other companies are publishing as "white papers." You'll be surprised at how low the bar is set and how you can easily exceed market expectations for good content.

  As you are calling each of your prospects and inbound leads, white papers are effective because they show that you are serious about the industry and that you are participating with thoughtful contributions.

  These papers also provide you with reasons to re-call prospects or inbound leads where your last call ended with a continuation instead of an advance. Remember those people that told you, "Yeah, send me over some stuff and I'll share it with the team"? Well, now you have real information and perspectives that you can send and ask for their opinion about what you wrote.

- Webinars/Webcasts: (I like the term "webcast" more, but that's just personal preference.) Hosting a webinar event is a very inexpensive way to reach your market, and it offers upstream/downstream market communication opportunities. Your webinars need not be a 60-minute dissertation dissecting your industry with marketing drop-ins throughout the presentation. Twenty minutes are all you need. Pick a current event and relate it to your industry.

  For example, the "Stop Online Piracy Act" (SOPA) legislation is a big topic of conversation across the Internet industry right now. Let's say you sell enterprise project management software. Your webinar title can be "SOPA & Enterprise Project Management." Develop a 10-slide presentation, spending 60-90 seconds per slide. Start the event on time and keep it to the time length you promised. Leave 3-5 minutes for Q&A and if no one asks a question, make up two questions and tell the audience, "Here's a question in the Chat Box from Margaret in Phoenix."

Any respectable webinar software platform (i.e., GoToMeeting) will log who has registered and attended, so now you have a two-part call list, those that attended and those that registered but did not attend.

You can repurpose this content by posting the recording to your blog and sending out to your contacts list with an email, "We hosted this webinar last week and I thought you'd like to watch the recording. We host these every month. Our next one is scheduled for November 10. Would you like me to reserve a seat for you now?" End with a question that makes the email personal, not marketing speak like, "…and if you'd like to register for next month's webinar, click here." That's marketing. We're selling here, which means that you must be personal with every interaction, not pretend personal.

I just rooted through my inbox and found this offer from a company that does memory storage and backup. (I have no idea how I ended up on their marketing list, but I digress.)

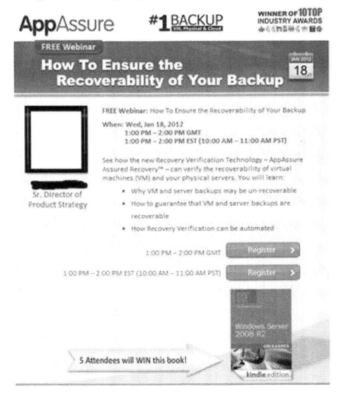

This particular approach feels a little too salesy. The main topic of the webinar is all about their company and product, which is a turn off for me. Also, while the person pictured in the email (whited-out) is probably a fantastic dude, but I'm not sure how including his picture adds much value. This seems like something a real estate agent or mortgage broker might do in an attempt to brand themselves.

> I do like the bullet points below the main text and how the time is clearly articulated with several calls to action and an incentive to attend. He may not get five people total to attend, but the suggestion that "only" five people will receive the book is a nice marketing tactic.

- Blog about your industry: This is an easy source of web traffic and shows your dedication to the industry. This will help your learning curve, providing you content and value to share with prospective clients as you develop your product and business. Writing also forces you to formulate ideas and opinions around industry topics. Use articles on industry-specific sites as fodder. Start your blog post with, "On Housing Wire today, it was announced that…" Then, write, "Here's another perspective…" Voila! Blog post and a voice (See Chapter 3 – "Find Your Voice.").

Know your industry-specific news sites. These industry news sites give you plenty of reasons to call a lead or a prospect to ask them how a particular happening affects their business. Develop a relationship with the writers and editors. Send them personal emails about perspectives on current industry issues. They will notice your expertise. Conclude your emails with, "Call anytime if you'd like a perspective for an article you're writing." Writers are always looking for quotes. This is free marketing and shows your expertise to the readership. It's another reason to blog and produce white papers – they reiterate your expertise for industry journalists.

Be a Connector

Usually this means networking and connecting people and it also means ideas. As

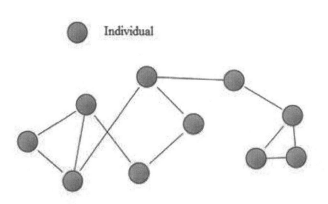

http://commons.wikimedia.org/wiki/File:Social-network.png

you are talking about the industry, by nature you become a communication hub for ideas. The "industry" could be hundreds, thousands, or millions of people. Here's a little secret – not everyone knows each other personally nor do they know what other people in the industry are thinking. As a self-developed communication hub, you develop the ability to establish connections between people and ideas. This is adding value.

Example: Connecting Ideas

In the housing industry right now, there is an ongoing conversation about the re-emergence of securitization, meaning that banks that make residential mortgage loans can package these loans into a large bundle called a Residential Mortgage-Backed Security (RMBS). (You might remember that these securitizations got out of control back in mid-2000s and contributed to the housing crash.) Principally, the idea of packaging loans and selling is a way for banks to mitigate lending risk. The industry is anxious to see when bank regulations will flush themselves out, making it possible for new RMBS issuances to emerge. I know, I know - a very stimulating topic. Here's the point: every trader, regulator, and analyst in the housing industry has opinion about this.

Whenever I'm calling someone that is involved with RMBS, I am asking their opinion. When I am reading industry publications, I'm searching for public positions and ideas on this topic that I can share. Then, when I make my next round of phone calls, the conversation presents value to the prospect.

> "Hi Roger. It's Scott Sambucci over at Altos Research. I've been reading about RMBS issuances this morning and just read an article on Housing Wire about how Company ABC projects that there will be at least five new RMBS issuances by Q4 of this year. I've been calling a few people that I know trade RMBS to see what they thought about this. Is that too aggressive? Feasible? What do you think?"

Maybe Roger gives you his opinion. And maybe by the end of the call, Roger says something like:

> "… so yeah, we're pretty optimistic. In fact, I'm working on a research report right now to present internally on this topic as we're setting our trading targets for the year."

Once you get that person's opinion, log the notes of your call in your CRM, distill it for yourself, and call the next person on your list:

> "Hi Ann. It's Scott Sambucci over at Altos Research. I've been reading about RMBS issuances this morning and just read an article

on Housing Wire about how Company ABC projects that there will be at least five new RMBS issuances by Q4 of this year. I've been calling a few people that I know trade RMBS to see what they thought about this. Is that too aggressive? Feasible? What do you think?"

When Ann gives you her opinion, you can say:

"That's interesting. I was just talking with another trader this morning that's working on some research on this area. I wonder if I should put the two of you in touch just so you can exchange a few ideas."

That's it; that's how you become a connector of ideas with yourself firmly planted as the cog for that information. Build with value.

Prospecting

This means scouring industry publications and emailing customers.

"Hi Bill - I saw this article on Housing Wire and immediately thought you'd find it interesting. How is this related to the work that you're doing on [insert topic]....?"

That's all, nothing fancy, just a way to start developing a voice and a place with your customers to engage and converse. The more you talk with your clients, the more opportunities they'll have to hear your voice. It is soooooo easy to set up your Google News Alert to gather these articles every day. Yet, no one does it, which is the opportunity for you to take advantage of everyone's "busy-ness" to cut through the day-to-day noise and become a beacon of light and knowledge. Spend 30 minutes each morning sending out 3-5 articles to specific contacts and prospects. Now, you are an information conduit, not just a salesperson or vendor.

An Over the Top Example of Adding Value

Katie works at a large homebuilder and has been a customer for a couple of years. It's a small account, but one we like to have because it is a notable company and they always pay for the year ahead of time. It's a nice little cash flow pop each year.

Katie and I hadn't spoken in several months. A few weeks ago, I saw an email that her company was expanding to a new market. I sent over a quick email congratulating them on the expansion and, of course, mentioned that we have some pretty awesome market data for that market. (Looking back, I should have picked up the phone - See Chapter 2 - "Pick up the Phone.") The good news is, whether due to my sending that simple note or otherwise, Katie emailed me a week later with a problem she was having.

Good morning Scott! I hope you are ready for the holidays!

We have been relying on your data for active listings in our Southern California markets. I am wondering if you track home closings or sales too. I am interested in increasing the integrity of the closing data I already have and would like to use another source.

Thanks for your assistance Scott.

My reply:

Hi Katie - We don't specifically have that info, but I have a couple of ideas/places where you might get this info. Can I call you Monday to discuss?

We talked on Monday and I first listened to the "why" behind her need. Turns out they are getting county assessor data from multiple sources, but it is still missing key data elements that they need. First, I suggested another company in our industry, a semi-competitor, but a reliable company that I know well. She appreciated that, but she said they weren't a good fit for this project. As we talked more, I realized that there was an opportunity to use the active market data she's already buying and how it's possible it could be matched with the transaction addresses. However, currently they were only buying slices of data in time, once in a quarter instead of a time series. She thought it might work, but had to think about the budget. Finally, I asked if she knew another company in the industry that had building permit data which might include the key fields she's looking for. She could cross-match addresses from the assessor's office with addresses in the permits. She hadn't heard of them, so I set up the email introduction. I know the guys at this company. I had met them several times at industry conferences. They are good people that I can trust passing along to her without brokering the communication. As a last follow up, the referred company released a press report on 12/16 and an industry blog reported on it. I saw it in my Google Reader later that day by chance. I sent that link to Katie to get her more acquainted with the index.

I did one more thing. I exported six months of data for Orange County, CA to her account so that she can run a trial match between the assessor data and our historical listing data. If it works, I'm sure she'll buy and I'll add an extra $1000 to the bottom line. If not, then it took all of five minutes to do this and I've added another tether to the relationship.

Remember:

Sales Tenet #8: Add value, add value, add value.

8 - Vampires & Gatekeepers

Sales Tenet #9: There is generally an inverse correlation between the amount of work the client expects you to do before the sale and the likelihood of the sale actually occurring.

A good prospect will say things like, "I think if we can run a test file or two and talk with you about how we would apply it to our daily workflow. That will provide us the insight we need to decide if this is a product we would want to implement."

Uneducated prospects will say things like, "Can you guys build out a custom model so that I can see if it will work in our system?" or "I'd like to run the sample files that we looked at last month to see how they've changed" or "I think that once I figure out exactly how we would use your product, we can come back to checking out your system in our next cycle." They don't understand the complexity of your product or the magnitude of the work that is required for what they perceive as a simple request. These people are Vampires.

Avoid Vampires. Your time is your primary currency as you start-up, so in the sales process you need to consider the opportunity costs of custom products, projects, and gatekeepers. Learn to say no, and learn to ask, "Why do you ask?" and "What do you want to accomplish?"

Vampires appear to be prospects but really aren't. They take the form of:

Image source:
http://commons.wikimedia.org/wiki/File:Little-vampire.svg

1. Nice guys that just want to be nice guys. They think they're doing you a favor talking to you. If a prospect asks, "Do you have some materials and pricing you can send over?" ask them, "When would you like to see this?" If they tell you, "It doesn't matter, whenever you have time" or "whenever you can get around to it", then you have a Vampire. There should a clear action step coming out of your conversation, with the client responsible for part of that action to show they are serious. If the prospect is not indicating urgency, that means you have not identified their critical business issue. Either the customer doesn't know they have a problem you can solve, the problem lacks urgency, or the person could be gatekeeping. You'll be calling that person for months to "follow up" with no results.

2. Lazy, er "busy," people. They are always looking to pilfer ideas, assume they have their system perfected, or think they don't need your product. They might like your product and concepts, but are too busy or too lazy to implement. Your product is priority #19 on list of two things they have to accomplish this quarter. These people will often talk with you and agree to stop by your booth or meet you at conferences.

3. Non-committal executives. They're executives because they usually know what they are doing. But, good executives also want their team to drive initiatives. They don't want to commandeer the ship too often unless you specifically articulate the reason they should dive into the weeds and promote your product. Instead, they expect you to do the leg work and the grunt work marketing and selling to his team. He'll dive deeper into the sales process when he's needed, which is usually at the end of the sales process, not the beginning.

4. Gatekeepers. These can be junior or senior executives, both usually seeking to hoard good ideas as their own and take the glory for them. You can use this motivation to your advantage, but this takes tremendous navigational skills. If you are an early stage company looking for early adopters, gatekeepers aren't worth your time. They aren't risk takers and will be a huge pain in the rear. Identify these people quickly, market to them, but do not cater to their whims. After a product demo, they'll say things like, "Okay, let me share this with the team and I'll get back to you" or "I'll have to spend more time with your system and if it makes sense, I'll present it to the team."

5. Oddly Enthusiastic. Alternately, beware of the overly enthusiastic prospect that promises to pass around your presentation and documentation to the entire team. You'll find this person shrouded in a statement like, "This sounds like exactly what we need! Can you forward me a presentation that I can share with the team?" even before he's seen a demo himself. If you forward your presentation and let him control the sales process, you're dead. They won't do what they say they will do. If they do, they'll literally hit the "forward" button on their email. It's too early for them to be a Product Champion. This takes time. Or worse, they do share your materials and completely botch questions they're asked, when you're not there. When you talk with them again, they'll say, "Yeah, we talked about your system as a team, but it's not a perfect fit right now. Keep us posted as things develop on your end."

If you have a Gatekeeper or an Enthusiastic, you have a couple of options:

1. Tell her, "That sounds great. Let's first do a walk-through of our XYZ software so you can see it in action. How about next Tuesday?" In setting up that demo, ask her to pull in a technical person to join her, saying "Who's the best person on your end to talk through any technical requirements, things like XML feeds and CSV data file transfers via FTP?" (This will test her technical prowess and also make her feel that it's okay to get other people helping.)

2. "Who would be the end user there?" If it's her, you have a legitimate chance of developing a Product Champion. If it's not her, you have a potential Gatekeeper that wants to present your product as a solution and take the credit. Ask her, "That's great. If you have 5-6 guys working the desk that will be the end users, who are the 1-2 people you trust to evaluate this with you?" To your Gatekeeper, it implies that you think she has control and that she's an influencer within the organization. She'll be more likely to bring in someone else.

Your primary objective is to get at least one other person with you on your next call. You need to elbow around in the organization and find more contacts. Each contact will offer more color and with each conversation, you can ask them for additional people that should get involved. Prior to the meeting, contact each person on the meeting invite to confirm the meeting. This is very professional and warrants getting more perspective prior to the presentation on hot buttons to push.

If you're worried about your Gatekeeper feeling a loss of control, call them first to confirm and, if you get voicemail, give yourself permission to contact the rest of the attendees:

> "Hi Bill. Thanks a million for our call tomorrow at 2 pm. You're going to love what you're going to see. I'm calling to confirm that you'll be dialing into the GoToMeeting line I provided in the meeting invite. I'll check with Mary and Tim, as well. Thanks again. Talk to you tomorrow at 2 pm Central."

When you do get 1-2 new people on the next call, they can often be silent. You must get them talking. Find out their role in the process. What makes them tick? How will your product influence their daily workflow? Many, many, many times the silent person is your Gatekeeper's manager. Your prospect (the Gatekeeper) squeezed their manager for 30 minutes to check out your totally awesome software. At the end of the call, this silent person will give the Roman "thumbs up – thumbs down" call on whether to proceed to the next stage of evaluation. If you don't sell to the silent people and their personal needs, you're dead because you've left the selling to your Gatekeeper, instead of controlling the sale yourself.

Example: New Lead

We recently had an initial call with a new prospect that was referred to us. We focused the call on situational questions, yielding these positive outcomes from the calls:

1. We had the COO and two senior product managers on the call on their end.
2. They patiently allowed us to ask our Situational questions.
3. After 5-6 of these questions, their COO jumped in and pointedly told us that their interest in the specific data product we've been discussing stemmed from 5-6 client requests they'd had in the last few months. Aha! He cracked!
4. They asked if they could see a demo of our product, which we did not do on this initial call. Remember:

Sales Tenet #2: Jumping into a sales demo on the first call is the kiss of death.

5. They agreed to send us a list of internal data that would be used in our system as a test case so they can see our software applied to a project they care about.
6. Our sales rep scheduled the next call for Wednesday at 2:00 pm Central.

What they didn't ask for that indicated they were a real prospect:

- "Send us the data we'll take a look."

- "Your system sounds interesting. Let us think about how we might use it and we'll get back to you [even though they've yet to actually see the product]."

- "Let's run this with 1000 of our portfolio properties and ask our clients if they like it. If they do, we can talk about a partnership of some kind."

Now, we know we have a genuine prospect. They've committed to a meeting and committed to doing work on their end by Friday. Our sales rep said that he would call them if he did not hear from them by Friday. They agreed. Whether they keep to that Friday schedule or if we hear back from them is yet unknown, though I strongly suspect we will. This is why getting the client to agree to do work is an excellent signal indicating their level of commitment to investigating your product or service. This is the difference between a prospect who is truly interested in your product and a prospect that is looking for free stuff or just browsing.

Inbound emails

Joe Carpenter planejock@earthlink.net via altosresearch.com

5:58 AM (3 hours ago)

to info

Greetings,

Your web site offers an opportunity to "look under the hood". I'd like to do just that. What do I need to do?

Thanks,

_Joe

My exchange with our sales rep:

Scott S. -

Have you reached out to this guy? Not sure if he's on the agent side or capital markets...

-John

Scott Sambucci

12/30/11 (2 hours ago) in reply to John

> *Nope - all yours. I would strongly recommend qualifying him well with his email address. Could be an individual investor just waiting to suck the life from your veins.*

He could be a very well-meaning person. A quick Google search of his name and email addresses yielded no results. Yes, he'll get a reply email, but if he doesn't bite or isn't willing to share more information, I'm moving on.

The reply to this email should be something like:

> *Hi Joe - Many thanks for the inquiry. Absolutely - we always love talking about our products.*
>
> *Because we've got many of them (products, that is) and so that we can talk about what's important for your work, tell me a bit more about yourself.*
>
> *Are you a Realtor, Broker, Individual Investor, or Wall Street tycoon? What brought you to Altos Research?*

End the email with open-ended questions so that he'll hit the 'reply' key and get back to you with more information. Meanwhile, I've checked our inbound registrations in our 'Leads' tab in Salesforce. He didn't register to the site. He's asking to look "under the hood" which is an offer we only make on our Capital Markets section of the site. Maybe he's somebody important, or maybe he's a Vampire with nothing to do but talk about cool products without any intention or budget to buy. I'll take my chances with engaging him in an email string instead of replying back with, "Oh, great! What time can I call you?" You owe it to yourself and your business to manage your time wisely.

Yes, be excited about every inbound lead. It's a pretty cool to think that some random person found your company and wants to know more. Just be smart about how you handle this exchange.

Bad News Brian

> *Hey Scott,*
>
> *I left a voicemail for Brian as I saw him in my pipeline and no one has reached out to him for a couple months. Any input from you on how to handle or what the status of that account is?*
>
> *Thanks,*
>
> *John*
>
> ----
>
> *Scott Sambucci*
>
> *11:00 AM (23 hours ago) in reply to John*

Run.

Why? Because the initial call was a referral from several months ago and the conversation revolved around a valuation product, which we didn't have. He continued to ask for another round of demos and discussion around how he could fit our round peg into his square hole of a problem. And worse, we obliged. We went round and round with three or four more demos anyway, included our Quantitative Analytics Director in the conversation to assist with model development and how to use the data. Adding up our calls, we spent 15-18 hours with this prospect. All that ended up being a 'no sale.'

"I thought we could get 100,000 records as a test"

We've had a few conversations with this lead. He's running a direct marketing company and would like to use our data to target specific consumers. His budget is tight. However, he's been forthcoming about this and so we constructed a purchase program that works for his budget. We shared the price and he verbally acknowledged that it would probably work. This all went down on Friday just before Christmas.

The next steps? He wanted to run a quick test of sample data to make sure the output is exactly what he needed. Sounds reasonable, so our sales rep reached out to him twice in the week between Christmas and New Year's Eve. Crickets. Until the afternoon of Friday, December 30th as everyone was packing up for the weekend. His assistant emailed to request 100,000 files for a test and wanted to get them before the end of the day.

Ahhhhh.... Now we see where this might be going. Here's where we are:

1. First, we're not releasing a file size that big as a test without a clear path to contract.
2. Processing a file that big takes a couple of days anyway.
3. We'd be willing to do that if we had a purchase order/contract squared away.
4. We've identified a potential Vampire.

The action we took?

"That's sounds great - we're excited that you're ready to go with the test.

Here's what we can do:

1. We'll request the sample data that you'd like to see for your test. Because this is such a large file, it'll take the weekend to process so we can kick that off today and probably have that ready on Jan 2.

2. *So that we can save time on implementation, I'll send over a contract to you with the terms that we've discussed. Let's get that signed and done. Then if the sample file is what you expected, we can roll immediately into providing you the updated data files right away."*

What does this do?

1. It determines if they are really serious or not. If they're serious, their response to this proactive project management will be, "Wow, that's a great idea! This will save us time to get things implemented once the test is finished."

2. It smokes out any underlying objections, if they resist, "Oh no, we're not ready to sign the contract yet." This opens the opportunity to ask, "Okay, what other questions do you have? Let's make sure we have them all answered before we avalanche you with these sample files."

This approach worked, sort of but not really. We signed up the client two months later after several rounds of price negotiation where we developed a "ramp up" pricing schedule for them. They paid less in the initial few months and then "ramped up" payments throughout the life of the agreement. During product implementation, we hit several rough patches where the customer asked questions about the product and began using our product in ways it wasn't intended. Six weeks into the agreement, they cancelled. While we earned some short term revenue from the work, the opportunity cost of time surely exceeded the dollars earned.

Remember:

Sales Tenet #9: There is generally an inverse correlation between the amount of work the client expects you to do before the sale and the likelihood of the sale actually occurring.

9 - Revenue Matters

Sales Tenet #10: Using a product and buying a product are very, very, very, very, very different.

Breaking the revenue seal matters. It is everything that makes or breaks your business. It shows that the market values your service and that prospects are not abusing your willingness to support them perpetually during an evaluation stage or beta test. Engaging in the revenue generation process forces your client to go through their internal RFP, approval, contracting, billing, and payment process. This will be revealing about your prospect's decision-making ability for the purchase.

Be confident. If your prospect is articulating the value of your product and its use for their organization, ask for their business. Still gun shy about this? Afraid to rock the boat? Think of it this way: would your prospect ask a prospective employee to work for free for a couple of weeks? Of course not. After the interview stage and decision to hire, the new employee begins receiving a salary. So should you.

If your prospect answers with "no" or "not yet" or "not right now" or "we don't have the budget" or "I'm not sure" or "let me see if I can get this approved," then they are not ready to spend money with you because you haven't completely shown the value of your product to solve a critical business need or you're dealing with the wrong

Image source:
http://commons.wikimedia.org/wiki/File:Indian_Head_Buffalo_Obverse.jpg

person. Keep selling. Start over with the sales process if you must. Re-ask situational questions to identify and to define their decision criteria and critical business issue. The decision criteria may have changed since initially interacting with your prospect three or six months ago. By asking for the business, you'll find out where you stand in the process and smoke out any underlying objections. There are many times that you'll discover you are much farther away from receiving a check than you think.

Here a few responses to your purchase questions that tell you exactly where you are in the sales process:

1. "<u>It's a little early for that yet. We still have a few other options that we're considering and haven't gotten as far evaluating them as we have with you.</u>" Surprise! You may have thought that you were close to the end decision. This response tells you that the prospect is still evaluating options instead of resolving final concerns before entering into a contract with you. This may be the first time you've heard that other solutions are on the table. Now, you can redefine criteria and really sell the key points and benefits of your product. Ask what other products they are evaluating and why these other products are under consideration. If they refuse to share this information you, that signals a weak relationship and means that there is other vital information they have not shared with you. Reset the sales conversation by confirming decision criteria again and reaffirming the situation and problems your prospect needs to solve.

2. "<u>Sure, send over the pricing details. It will help me out with requesting a budget.</u>" This response tells you that the customer is the first of several decision layers at the target account and it tells you that this expense is probably a new one. You now have a "double sale" to tackle. The first sale is on your product ("Does it solve their problem?"), and the second is selling internal channels on a new expenditure ("Can we pay for it?"). In this second part of the sale, you'll be hitting fundamental cost-benefit questions with the bean counters, managers, and legal counsel, so be prepared to sell all over again from the start (See Chapter 10 – "Negotiation & Contracts"). This latter group of people may only be vaguely familiar with your product (if at all) and you can assume that they haven't thought through the intricacies of a complete cost-benefit analysis.

3. "<u>I usually don't handle the expenses and budgets. I'll have to see who the person is that does.</u>" This tells you that your prospect is not a decision-maker. If they were, they would know exactly how

to gain approval for the purchase because they would have gone through this budget approval process at least once before with a previous purchase. This is an important finding because you now must find out who this person's manager (and often their manager) is and begin selling to them.

As a start-up, begin the revenue process as early in your product development cycle as possible. The process of migrating a 'user' to a 'customer' will reveal the answers to several vital questions about your business and its viability. For startups, Eric Reis refers to the release of an MVP, a "Minimal Viable Product." Developing an MVP is not just important to deliver a solution that you think the market will accept, but also introduces you and your prospect to the required process involved with the purchase of your product.

In "Selling Into a New Market," Brian Burns discusses how to manage the technical and business sale simultaneously. This is an excellent method of testing how serious your prospect is about purchasing your product instead of lingering in evaluation purgatory. The premise? Each sale has a "technical sale" (to the users of your product) and a "business sale" (to the managers and bean-counters). The technical users have to accept that the product will markedly improve their work life to justify its expense. The business sale requires you to highlight this value in dollars and cents, so the managers approve it. By engaging in both processes simultaneously, you can determine the seriousness of your prospect. If your prospect gives you access to the business team, they are clearly serious about implementing your product upon a successful evaluation. If not, you run the risk of winning the technical sale, and starting all over again with presentations and objections to win the business sale. Alternately, you might have an executive-level Product Champion ready to approach the business sale, only to be vetoed by his technical team because they feel your product fails to meet their requirements. Work both together to save time and to determine which of your prospects are real and which are Vampires.

Questions to Ask Yourself & Your Prospects

Here are a few questions to ask about your product and revenue generation:

1. <u>Is my target user able to approve the budget expenditure, and where does your product fit into the user's budgeting process?</u> By seeking revenue, you'll find out if the target user (the mid-level manager) is capable of approving the $5000/month budget amount herself, or if she needs to go up the ladder to her manager or the Division president. If so, you may be required to host a second (or third or fourth...) sales presentation to the user's manager or

Division head. That person will likely have a completely different set of decision criteria requirements to meet and objections to overcome before approving the order. In this third or fourth sales demo, you might see the Division President turn to your Product Champion and ask, "Okay, so why should we buy this? How will it help you?" The president is testing to see if your prospect is really dying to use your product, or if they're just caught up in the sexiness of your product's interface. The Division President is tearing through the veneer to be sure that your user will solve a critical business issue with your product. It's the ultimate "sink or swim" for your sale.

Many companies have specific time cycles and budgets allotted for new purchases. If your project management software is not a replacement for an existing cost and your target user doesn't have budget available, you may end up waiting until next quarter or next year before you can actually complete the transaction. Be ready to offer flexible payment terms in these cases, such as delayed billing (See Chapter 10 – "Negotiation & Contracts"). Offering this option will expose whether "budget" is the real objection or if there's something else festering beneath the surface that your prospect hasn't yet shared or emphasized.

In the sales process, you'll be able to start identifying Gatekeepers versus decision-makers. This is HUGE when it comes to understanding opportunity pipeline projections from introduction to closed sale.

2. <u>What legal, contract, and due diligence requirements are needed?</u> You might be expecting that you can send over an invoice (or even an email) and expect it to be paid by the user. Or, you are expecting the user to charge the expense to a credit card and expense it on their own budget. Or maybe you haven't thought about this at all and are hoping your Paypal account will do. Instead, the user's company likely requires a list of due diligence requirements from you including proof of up-time, server security, and protection of any proprietary information shared in your software. The user's company might require a license agreement and contract, even if you're not requiring one. These all add overhead to your customer acquisition costs. Think about this from a project management and time management standpoint.

3. <u>Is the product priced correctly?</u> Your free users during beta stage told you time and time again that they'd "easily be willing to spend the $5000/month for your totally awesome product." Now, they

are balking. Too many start-ups depend on hypothetical questions with regard to pricing. You cannot depend on what people say, only on what they do. The only way to validate a price is to actually sell the product at that price. Alternately, you might have every new customer tell you, "Wow! $5000? That's it? Send me the invoice and I'll have that paid by bank wire transfer in two days!" Then, for your next batch of leads, move your asking price up to $7500 or $10,000.

<u>Can you sell to the other 95% of adopters?</u> In every industry, there are early adopters that always use the latest and greatest innovations. By selling to these early adopters, you'll start to see patterns in their objections or even hear comments like, "I love your software. A lot of people I talk to at other companies might want to see more features or have problems with such-and-such functionality that you have, but I can work around it." This reveals potential objections from the mass audience that you ultimately need to reach in order to explode sales. Early adopters might view your product as a nice "add-on" to the tool set and have the budget to pay for it. However, the rest of the market won't have the budget for an "add-on" product, nor will they be willing to spend the time implementing a product that isn't perceived as core to their daily work. Look for these signals as you are selling to early adopters, so that you can address them with the rest of the market.

Publicity photo of journalist Mike Wallace for the television program *Mike Wallace Interviews*.
http://upload.wikimedia.org/wikipedia/commons/8/8b/Mike_Wallace_Interviews_1957_%281%29.jpg

<u>Is your product a "nice-to-have" or "gotta-have"?</u> Money talks, but sometimes it's not about the money. It's about the implementation costs and resources required. You envision that the customer says, "Yes!" to the contract and, poof! Magically, your software is installed and the three key users immediately begin using it with grand success. Because of your software, they now only work four hours a day, spend the extra time with their wife and kids, and because of you they earned a bonus so they can take the two-week African safari they've been dreaming about for years. Guess what? It doesn't work that way.

If your totally awesome product requires regular updates or some level of hardware or personnel to maintain, your product doesn't cost $5000/month to the customer. It costs much more.

Until you get through the implementation process and have the users completely trained and utilizing your product every day, the sale is not complete. More so, you are ignorant to all of the factors weighing into your prospect's decision to make the purchase. You must factor these implementation costs into your price for the long term sustainability of your business.

Many times the implementation process reveals landmines in your product and service. It's not until the local systems integration manager begins installing your product that technical hurdles are noticed. Every client will be different and many clients will not have IT people with the same motivation and interest in proper implementation as your Product Champion and you. In fact, the local IT people may see your product as *extra* work, especially when they have to upgrade their system software or hardware to properly implement your product.

4. "Based on our conversations, we've covered [enter defined decision criteria here]. Can you think of any other outstanding questions before I put together our work agreement and we can begin the purchase process?" A specific example:

You: "Based on our conversations since we met at the Enterprise Software Conference, we've covered how our ABC software enables you to keep an extra administrative headcount off the books, increase your batch processing time, and turn around customer support requests at least two hours faster than your current system, a 400% improvement. Can you think of any other outstanding questions before I put together the working agreement so we can begin the purchase process?"

Prospect: "Nope, I think that's it."

You: "That sounds great. Do you have a standard vendor agreement that your company prefers to use?"

Always go this route first, because by using their paperwork, you avoid the legal review of your homegrown contract. (See Chapter 10 – "Negotiations and Contracts".) More importantly, this will tell you if your prospect knows how to buy products from outside vendors. If they respond with, "Jeez, I don't know. I'll have to figure out who to ask about that" then you know you have more work to do.

Saying no to Big Earls

In my consulting days, I spent six months pre-selling my services leading up to an international trade event hosted in San Diego. The Embassy of Kazakhstan organized a trade summit between US and Kazakh companies and government leaders. Because my company focused on establishing and developing these types of relationships, the event was a prime opportunity to develop a set of clients on both sides early in my company's life.

One of the US companies was a manufactured housing company based in Chula Vista (just outside of San Diego), "Big Earl's" company. (I call him Big Earl because he was a gruff, portly man, the kind of guy that saw business transactions as bar fights.) In helping to promote the conference in the US, I gained access to the list of firms interested in attending. When Big Earl showed interest in the event, I contacted him to answer his questions and to prime him for consulting work. Earl and I hit it off marvelously and after a phone call or two, we decided it made sense for me to spend the day with him to understand their business and logistics of doing business in Kazakhstan.

I jumped on a flight to San Diego (on my own dime) and spent the day with Earl. After the first hour of our meeting, I was introduced to the company owner. Oops… I mistakenly thought and assumed that Earl was the man in charge. Now, I had another layer to sell. We talked through the opportunities and pulled out a map to talk through shipping options for materials from the US to Kazakhstan. Big Earl sported a classic 6-series BMW and treated me to a wonderful lunch at a fancy restaurant. Things were going along swimmingly as I ignored the signals early in the relationship.

At the event, I established meetings between Earl and the key Kazakh government ministers. This included translation services while my Kazakh business partner sat with him in meetings to help Earl show well to the ministers. The meetings went great and Earl was excited about the opportunities.

In the afternoon, we had a break in the action so Earl, my Kazakh partner, my US partner, and I sat down for a pow-wow. We asked Earl how things were going and he couldn't hide his excitement. We said, "Wow, that's great. So, what happens next?" Earl proceeded to talk about timelines and shipping and all of the fantastic work we were going to do.

We asked him, "That's great Earl! So, when do we start getting paid?" That wasn't exactly a question Earl wanted to hear. He sternly replied, "You get paid when I get paid." We were talking about 6-, 12-, and 18-month timelines here, at least. Earl expected us to help him out all along, organize the logistics, manage the customs paperwork, and develop the business locally in Kazakhstan, which would open the opportunity for him to sell his product. Then and only then we would begin receiving payment. Huh? That was the last time we spoke with Big Earl.

Here are the mistakes I made:

1. When I hopped on the plane on my own dime to visit Earl before the conference, I signaled that I was working with him as a partner, not as a value-adding service provider.
2. At the initial on-site meeting, I should have laid out a fee schedule to him and negotiated terms, weekly, monthly, and project rates.
3. I failed to qualify Big Earl's role as a decision-maker.

Customers intentionally or unintentionally will take advantage of you. Earl was doing so intentionally and I let him get away with it from the beginning. Other customers will do this unintentionally, either thinking that the long ramp up and testing periods are part of your normal sales cycle, or they know that you are a new company in the industry and they think they're doing you a favor as a user. It is your responsibility to the customer, your company, and yourself to generate revenue and articulate the steps to getting there.

Example: Big Hedge Fund

We initiated a sales process with a very large hedge fund. Because they've been burned in the past from vendors that have over-promised and under-delivered, they asked us produce a custom report on specific product performance metrics. This was a legitimate request and very different from the client asking for us to export all of the data and saying, "let us use it for 6 months and we'll tell you if it's useful. If it is, then we can talk about a contract." Now, the problem is that creating this custom report would take about two days of coding time and a day of computing time, substantial resources for our company.

Before going down this road, we hosted a phone call with our product sponsor at the fund to find out:

1. <u>What are their benchmarks? What percentages and performance metrics are acceptable?</u> The prospect didn't know the answer to this question! There were no other competitive products or industry benchmarks. This meant that we could have a 95% success rate, but the prospect could arbitrarily decide that it needs to be 100% without understanding that 100% would be impossible to reach. They wanted to view the evaluation results and decide if the rates were something they could work with, yet they weren't working with anything now. See the circular argument in this?

2. <u>What other outstanding questions do you have with respect to the product?</u> We needed to know if we were in the final stages of the decision process, or at stage 2 of 20 or stage 17 of 20. This question uncovered a critical point in the sales process. The prospect told us, "It's too soon to tell. Once I have all the materials from you, then I need to present it to my managers. They might have questions that I haven't thought of yet." Aha! So the person who we thought was the decision-maker really wasn't, at least not on his own.

3. <u>If we can get this to you by next week and the numbers are acceptable, will we be able to initiate the agreement process?</u> This is an excellent trial close to smoke out any lingering objections. If the answer was "yes," we'd be happy to spend the time and resources to deliver the requested diagnostics. If not and they replied with, "No, actually we have some other questions" then we've smoked out other objections to overcome before allocating the coding time.

In this particular case, because question #2 showed us that we were far earlier in the process than we thought, we skipped question #3. But, if the answer to question #2 was something like, "I can't think of anything else" then question #3 is a trial close to be doubly sure that there aren't any other lingering objections. If the response to this question is, "Nope, I think we'll be good" then you follow up with, "Okay great. While we're putting together the diagnostics you requested, we can work on the agreement in parallel to save time. Do you have a vendor agreement that you prefer to use?"

Tracking Payments

Just so you know, tracking and receiving payments from customers generally sucks. You may have to develop your inner "Vito the Collections Guy." You can do everything right on your end, send the invoice, confirm receipt, provide wiring instructions, and answer every question that your prospect's accounts payable person has. Despite all that, invoices do not always get paid in a timely way, or at all, nor do your prospects always know how to resolve these situations. Always, always, always find out from your new customer who the main point of contact is for you on the accounting side. If possible, organize a ten minute phone call with your prospect, their accounts payable person, and yourself just to talk through the payment process. This will make your invoice memorable, curtail side tracks, and it might be the first time ever that your prospect actually talked to their accounts payable person.

We had a challenge with a very large existing customer that went through a corporate spin-off. They had paid reliably every month for more than two years until the corporate split. As a result of the split, no one in the company knew who was responsible for paying vendor invoices now. It took three (yes, three!) months of phone calls and emails to find this person. It happens, so be ready.

Here's a great question to ask, "So that we don't have to bother you with accounting questions, who is the best point of contact for payments?" PICK UP THE PHONE and develop a relationship with that person. This person will be the lifeblood of your existence with your new customer.

Remember:

Sales Tenet #10: Using a product and buying a product are very, very, very, very, very different.

10 - Negotiation & Contracts

Sales Tenet #11: Always tell the truth so you never have to remember what you said.

Congratulations! You've received commitment from the end user and team. Now, you are engaged with the legal, due diligence, and implementation team.

A few rules on negotiation:

Image: Library of Congress, Broadside Collection, portfolio 169, no. 27 c-Rare Bk Coll.
REPRODUCTION NUMBER: LC-USZ62-40873
http://hdl.loc.gov/loc.pnp/cph.3a41202 (Source: http://commons.wikimedia.org/wiki/File:The_Four_Traitors.jpg)

1. <u>Tell the truth so you don't have to remember what you said</u>. You are selling a new product as a new company in your industry. Don't be a douchebag by telling your prospect one price early in the sales process and then jacking it up, because you think you quoted them too low. It is acceptable to change your price based on new information, which is why is it is vital to provide summary notes of every call and articulate for your clients the difference between the initial quote and the new one, "Yes, back in August we did say

that the annual license would be $25,000 for our Economy product for all three users. However, since then, we've been evaluating our Premier product for twenty users, which is why we're looking at $150,000, now."

2. <u>Develop a road map or flowchart of the negotiation process and pivotal conversations</u>. Sketch this out on a white board before a big call. Think ahead of questions and options that your customers might request.

For example, let's assume you've been discussing a site license that includes 15 seats for your prospect's entire team. You should prepare the answers to these questions:

- What if your prospect asks for 3 or 5 (or 50!) licenses instead? How will that affect pricing?

- What if your client comes back at you with a price proposal that is a third (or a tenth!) of what you quote? How will you respond?

- How will you offer any adjustments to the price without appearing to be price cutting, such as a quarterly payment via bank wire transfer instead of monthly invoices?

- What if your customer requests a 30-day cancellation clause at any time throughout the agreement instead of committing to a full year term?

You must think about these iterations ahead of time, so you can work through the major agreement issues in a calm, natural, and professional way during the call. Be prepared.

You will not always work through every single question or objection in a single call. That's okay. The goal is to identify outstanding questions, so you can progress the negotiation and finalize in a subsequent call, if needed. Certainly, try to resolve these items in one call if you can and having a flowchart on a white board will help you move through more of the process on the initial call. Ultimately, treat the contract process as you would a sale in itself. Your prospect's legal team will have questions, objections, and expect some concessions. Clearly articulate their questions in your own words, confirming that you have their questions understood. Treat them like a checklist. Once you reach the end the checklist, your contract process should be finished.

3. <u>Ask your Product Champion for help in preparing for the call with his attorneys</u>. Ask him, "What sort of questions does your legal team typically ask? What are the concessions they usually request?" At this point in the sale, he's as invested in the process as you are and wants to see this project gain approval. Frequently his reply will be something like, "Oh boy, they ALWAYS ask for a 30-day opt out" or "In every contract, they always start with slicing the price quote by 50%, even when I tell them that we've already been through the price agreement conversation." Now, you have a heading for your call prep and flowchart.

4. <u>Be flexible but consistent on pricing</u>. I know you want to finalize the deal, but if you start creating arbitrary prices and discounts to finalize agreements with individual clients, you'll regret it down the road. Need an example? I thought you might…

   We provided a super-duper discount to a customer to get a deal done a couple of years ago. He was happy and wonderful. Then, he moved companies. He wanted to buy our service at his new job and we quoted him our normal price, which was 400% what he was paying at his old job. Guess what? He freaked. He had already told his new director all about our product, how awesome it was and how much it costs, all before picking up the phone to call us to place an order with no selling involved. That was a tough conversation to have, because he had to go back to his director at his brand new employer and ask for 400% of the budget already approved. Think he felt like a boob in front of his new boss?

   If you do offer a tremendous discount or highly favorable terms, document it for your customer and in your account notes. You never want to look back months or years later and say, "Huh? Why is this monthly payment $1000/month when our going rate is $5000/month?"

5. <u>Be prepared to act quickly and then be ready for a protracted contract, due diligence, and negotiation process</u>. Your Product Champions might expect that the contract will take "a week or two." This can easily turn into a month or two or three or four. Be proactive throughout the cycle and be very nice to corporate attorneys and vendor managers. After each conversation, send a summary email with both resolved and outstanding questions. This develops a checklist for both sides to view during the process. Find the LinkedIn profiles of the attorneys, vendor managers, and accounts payable people just like you did with your prospect. Everyone is part of the sale.

"OK – Send me over a quote"

If you hear this, you haven't finished selling. Earlier in the sales process, you should have discussed approximate pricing based on the product and service that you are providing with your prospect. This conversation generally happens between the first couple of calls and the point when your Product Champion and team begin hammering you with final objections and questions about support and implementation. Discussing price is part of the qualification process. It is YOUR responsibility to initiate this part of the sales discussion if it appears that the client appears to be ignoring the topic. Don't pretend everything is okay. It's not okay if you haven't discussed price at a reasonable point in the sales process.

Here are some questions that you can use either earlier in the sales process to initiate this conversation, or later in the process if you did not get there first time around:

- "What's the approval process for a purchase like this?" This tests a few key aspects of the sale. First, it will indicate to you if your contact is indeed a decision-maker. Sometimes your contact becomes squirrely. If they answer with, "Oh, I make all the decisions" or "Eventually I'll run it up the flagpole, but I'm be leading the initial product evaluation for now" you might be in trouble with a Vampire or Gatekeeper. Yes, there are times when a single person in a company is able to make a unilateral decision and has the budget. This is very, very rare. Do not fool yourself into a false sense of optimism that you've now completed your sales process due diligence. Or, they might say, "I don't know. I have to figure out how we're going to pay for this."

- "Are you planning to allocate this to your budget or cost-share with your IT department?" This is an indirect way of asking whether your prospect has the budget and the ability to make a decision on their own. If they are planning to cost-share, know that you may need to dive back into the sales process with a second team to run through another set of demonstrations that includes asking situational questions, defining criteria, and illustrating how your product solves a critical business issue for the second team.

- "While I know you're not yet at a point to make your final decision to begin using the product, it probably makes sense to provide you with some pricing guidance. How about we review a few pricing options to make sure we're all on the same page?" Your prospects will respect you for this and you will find out much earlier in the sales process whether you have a qualified prospect. (See Chapter 8 – "Vampires & Gatekeepers".) Almost always your prospect will say, "That's a good idea. So, how much is it?" Then, you can begin the discussion. You might quote $10,000/month and your prospect replies with, "Hmmm... We have $5000 budgeted for this project and that includes another unrelated product we need to purchase." Great! Now, you know that they have budget for this expenditure and how much is available. You can then tailor a solution to match the budget available before reaching the end of the sales process and having it completely deflate because you didn't discuss pricing earlier.

Example Conversation

With this example conversation early in the sales process, your objective is to make sure that you and your prospect are in the same relative price area. You need to make sure your prospect isn't thinking that the price is $1,000 a year, if the actual price is $100,000 or $150,000. If you are having this conversation later in the sales process, be prepared to walk through a variety of options and paths to reach a mutual agreement.

> You: "While I know you're not yet at a point to make your final decision to begin using the product, it probably makes sense to talk through the transaction side of things. How about we review a few pricing options to make sure we're all on the same page?"

Prospect: "That's a good idea. How much is a site license?"

You: "Sure. Let's recap what we know so far. You have 15 people on your team that will need a seat license, and you'll want to have a manager's account, so that you can view everyone's activity in a summary report each week. Does that sound right?"

> > This assures that you and the prospect are in agreement with the expected use and you are ending with a question that requires active participation from the prospect. This should be a conversation, not a presentation or a pitch. Relax, it's just a business transaction.

Prospect: "Yeah, pretty close, though I don't think we'll need one for all 15 people. I'm thinking we'll probably only have 10-12 users."

You: "OK, that makes sense. We can always add more seats as we go. Is there anything else that you can think of in terms of users or licenses?"

> > Here, you are confirming that there are no add-ons that the client is expecting. This is very, very important, because later in the

transaction as you are finalizing the deal, prospects will often ask for a few 'throw-ins', "Oh, you know what, I totally forgot, but we'll need three licenses for the IT team so they can prepare reports for the team. Can you just include that in the price we agreed to?" Asking this question early in the sales process gives you cover to respond to these 'throw-in' requests with, "We can definitely add three more licenses, though they will be a little extra above what we agreed to last month."

Prospect: "OK, sounds good. I can't think of anything else right now."

You [speaking slowly, clearly, and confidently]: "Great, here's a summary. A manager's license is $2500 per year and the user seat licenses are $1500 per user per year. With 10 users, that comes to $152,500 for a one-year license for your team. Again, that's 10 users at $1500 each and your manager account which is $2500, which is how we arrive at $152,500."

> Yes, repeat yourself to make sure they heard you. Their cell phone may have just buzzed with a text message or they could have dropped their pen. Once you've repeated the quote, immediately be quiet. Don't speak, don't talk. Even if the prospect is quiet. Let them think about it. Your prospect could be scribbling notes, doing back-of-the-envelope math, or whispering to their operations manager sitting with them on the call. Just be still. They're not going anywhere and they didn't hang up the phone.

<u>A Few Possible Prospect Responses and How to Handle:</u>

<u>Response #1</u>: "That's a lot more than I expected."

> This might be a true statement, it might be a negotiating tactic, or it might be reactionary. Do not take this personally. This is not an insult to your company, your product, or you. Remember, this is just a business transaction.

You: "Okay, let's talk about that. What did you have budgeted for this purchase?"

<u>Response #2:</u> "We don't have any budget for this. We're trying to see what's out there to see if this is purchase we want to make" or "I wasn't sure what to expect."

> This tells you that you are still early in the sales process, because your prospect has not yet presented a case to management for budget allocation for this purchase. They are still evaluating

options, which might include 1) your product, 2) another product, 3) building a product themselves, or 4) doing nothing. Just based on those four options, you're now at a 25% probability of getting the sale, and that is before the rest of the sales process is complete, while each stage might chip away at that 25%.

You: "Sure, I understand. What is that process like?" Your prospect might say:

Prospect: "Well, I've been priming my manager for a few months that this is something we need. I'm pretty sure I can get this approved. How much flexibility is there on the price?"

> Now, you know you have a real prospect who is willing to go to bat for you internally. You can openly begin negotiating with trial closes:

You: "I think there's some. What did you have in mind?" (or "What were you thinking?" or "What works with your budget?")

Prospect: "Well, what about somewhere around $100,000 for all of the licenses, plus three additional for the IT team?"

You: "I think we can do that. If I can get my partner to agree, are we good?" (Personally, I don't like using the "do we have a deal?" because it sounds too salesy.)

Prospect: "Yep, we do."

You: "Great. Hold on a second and let me grab Bob to make sure we can do that." Put your hand over the receiver, sing Happy Birthday or a couple of rounds of 99 Bottles of Beer on the Wall, and take a deep breath, smile into the phone and say, "Okay we're good."

Response #3:

Prospect: "I'm not sure. I'll have to look over these numbers and see if this is something I want to present to the rest of the team. (And by 'team,' he means 'my manager'.) Can you send me over the PowerPoints, so that I can present this internally?"

> You know where to go with this from Chapter 6 – "More Sales Process."

Response #4:

Prospect: "I'm not sure. Let me think about it and I'll get back to you."

> Gulp. Your prospect just told you that they are not interested, ready to buy, or able to afford it. Right here, right now, you absolutely positively must resuscitate the sale.

You: "Tell me more about what you're thinking." Get the prospect to talk. Your objective right here is to find out why you are now getting stonewalled. Was the price waaaaay too high for this person to approve? Were they only toe-dipping from the beginning? Did you fail to uncover a critical business issue?

If they resist telling you more, then you need to be honest –

You: "Here's why I'm asking. We've had a couple of very productive phone calls. You told me that in order for your business unit to make its Q1 revenue goals, you need to increase the call volume they are handling. The product we've been reviewing together will increase you call volume handling by a minimum of 35%, which translates to approximately $1,500,000 in new revenue for you. A $150,000 investment yields you a 10x return just in Q1 alone. Help me understand your decision process some more." Now, you are back in the sales process and asking questions to identify needs and establish decision criteria.

Response #5: "Your competitor's product is less than a third of your price."

> Okay, this is a really annoying, because you know that either there is not a head-on competitor for your product or your competitor's product is deficient, which is why you decided to build your product in the first place. It's also dejecting to think that after all of the time and work invested, the decision is shrouded as a price-based decision. But, the good news is that now you have a clearer picture of objections to overcome and places where you can differentiate your product for your prospect versus other options he has.

"OK – Send me a contract"

Two strategies:

1. <u>Turn it around</u>. "Joe, I can definitely do that. Here's a thought. You guys are a bigger organization with corporate attorneys that get paid a lot of money. In my experience, the approval process will be smoother and quicker if you send over your vendor agreement and I'll just fill in the details of what we're doing together."

   If your buyer hasn't bought from vendors before, this might present a challenge to them. They won't know where to get this agreement. So be flexible. If you notice ANY hesitation on this, just move on to #2.

2. <u>Send your generic contract</u>. Why? It keeps the momentum of the sale going. Additionally, when your customer sends the contract to legal, their legal team will happily either mark-up your contract so that it meets their internal criteria, or they'll scrap it and give your customer the company's vendor agreement for you to sign. This can turn out to be the best method to moving things quickly because now you're using their contract and making the attorneys look smart. They like that.

If you don't have a contract, go to DocStoc.com and find a template you can use. After you send out two or three contracts to various prospects, you'll see a pattern emerge of common changes and additions that you can add as standard (or purposely omit to use as negotiating concessions).

More on Pricing – Vendor Managers

Be firm and transparent on price. Some companies have vendor managers shrouded as attorneys. They will take your contract with all of the terms you've agreed to with your customer and then begin a new negotiation process. I've had this happen with a very large investment bank. After working with the trading desk for several months on test files, reviewing products, and agreeing to terms on price, delivery, and duration, I was introduced to Martha during the contract phase. Martha's job was a vendor manager whose job is to negotiate contracts with vendors. After sending our flimsy contract, I was returned their standard vendor agreement. Martha took the terms of our contract and pasted them into their agreement. We reviewed the agreement point by point and reached the last section detailing price and delivery. She said, "Okay, so let's talk about the price." Huh? I'd already gone through this process with the end users, the trading desk, and had already put together a nice deal for them based on certain concessions they requested. I thought we were good to go. No one informed Martha this, nor had an incentive to do so. In her mind, the traders didn't care about price and bought everything that they wanted. It was her job (and later I learned she was measured on this) to negotiate discounts and favorable payment terms (i.e., net-90 instead of 'due on receipt.')

Martha: "What can you do with the price?"

Me: [Gulp. Was this going to be a deal breaker?] "What do you mean?"

Martha: "Let's work on this price a little."

Me: "Martha, this is the price of the product that is being purchased. Let me explain why..."

In this case, I started with our standard list pricing (set a high anchor price) and showed how the price included in the contract included a 25% discount from our list price because of this and that. I think she was disappointed that she missed out on the negotiating fun, but ultimately understood where we were. Looking back, I should have avoided this by asking the users about the contract process earlier in the sales conversation. They might have told me, "Oh yeah, we have a Vendor Relations department that handles all of the contract mumbo jumbo." From there, I could have asked if the Vendor Relations Department handled budgeting and pricing, or if that stayed resident with the user group. Who knows? Maybe I would have learned nothing from these questions, and if I learned something by asking, I would have been better prepared for the conversation with Martha.

Corporate Attorneys are People Too

Image: John Breckenridge, Attorney General of the United States under Thomas Jefferson. http://upload.wikimedia.org/wikipedia/commons/3/3c/John_Breckinridge%2C_Attorney_General.jpg

Remember the people that you're working with at this stage are often corporate attorneys. Most of them are really, really nice people that are also really, really smart. They're not out to add "gotcha" ticks to their wall. They're just paid a lot of money to ardently protect their employer, so you need not take their comments, suggestions, and negotiations personally. Also, remember that most corporate attorneys have little or no experience with the product or business development side of their company. They may not even really understand what their own company does, the problem it solves, and how or why their company makes money. (Yes, this is a massive over-generalization, but you get the point. Corporate attorneys are not sitting in front of their customers building or pitching products.)

Contract Versions & Call Summary Notes

Make life easy for attorneys and they will make life easy for you. You're going to have several back-and-forth emails and phone calls throughout the process. Attorneys like to work in Microsoft Word so they can mark changes in the document. Retain a copy of each revision and include a time and date in each file name. Trust me on this one.

For example:

ABC_Corp_YourCompany_License_Agreement_2012-01-19_815am

ABC_Corp_YourCompany_License_Agreement_2012-01-21_945am

ABC_Corp_YourCompany_License_Agreement_2012-01-22_230pm-FINAL

Take really, really good notes of every call, summarize your notes in a well-formatted email, send them to the other party, and ask for their agreement on your notes by ending your emails with a question, "Anything else from our conversation that I may have missed?"

Remember:

Sales Tenet #11: Always tell the truth so you never have to remember what you said.

11 - Be Nice & Eat Your Broccoli

Sales Tenet #12: Be nice. Always, always, always be nice.

This is a rule of life. Be nice all of the time, without exception, to everyone you meet. This includes taxi cab drivers, front desk managers, airline attendants, the retail clerks, waitresses, and your family. Everyone is out there doing their own thing. They all have a reason for being where they are right now, whether they are there in a good mood, bad mood, or somewhere in between. Ask people earnestly, "How's it going today?" Not, "Hi. How are you?" as you trail off to a question about whether the French fries are thick cut or thin cut. Really ask them, "Wow, it looks like it's crazy busy in this place today. How's it going?" Speak human and be human. It matters, especially when you're having a crappy day. And, you'll feel a whole lot better when you're nice to other people.

Image: http://commons.wikimedia.org/wiki/File:Don%27_worry,_be_happy.jpg

Why being nice matters for business, too

In December, I had a long conversation with an analyst at a very large bank. He and I have been working together for more than a year to discover applications for our data products in his predictive modeling. Check out how I came to work with John:

1. How did I find John? From blog post comment he left last year.

2. How did he find me? From his new colleague, Jim, that joined his team.

3. Where did come Jim from? An inbound call in June 2009, when he was exploring the start of a hedge fund seven states away from where he lived and worked now.

4. How did Jim find us? He registered on our company website after seeing a blog post referring to an article published in Forbes magazine using our housing data back in 2007. (See Chapter 3 – "Find Your Voice")

Our company receives phone calls every week from investors and individuals starting hedge funds. Starting a hedge fund is no easy task, though the newbies trying it may think it is. We've seen most of these new funds never get off the ground, but as a part of their research process they need to understand what data is available to them so they can build a case to their potential investors about the informational advantage they will have in their investment process. It is very easy to bristle when receiving these inbound calls because they almost never lead to any business for us and for those that do, they are a high opportunity cost because of the inordinate amount of service and support required for these small accounts. But, I always, always, always tell myself to be nice to these inbound callers. They are out there bird-dogging a new idea and pursuing it. Who am I to be snarky or assume they can't make it? So, I was nice to Jim, and went two years before I heard from him again via my initial call with John the Analyst, who said, "I heard about you guys from Jim Smith who just joined us." This was the same guy who was trying to start a hedge fund back in 2009! How about that?

During the course of the conversation, John the Analyst asked me if I had heard about his bank's new program related to their asset portfolio. This new program presented a very large opportunity for our company. A key person heading this initiative was a person to whom I was referred to by another vendor, who I called to talk with about a white paper that he wrote and published. This vendor and I hit it off and established a pleasant working relationship, including this second vendor referring me to key personnel that he works with at other large institutions. All this happened because I was nice.

Read Books Everyday

Image source: http://commons.wikimedia.org/wiki/File:Broccoli_and_cross_section_edit.jpg

News articles, magazines, and TechCrunch don't count. They are important for daily reading and to identify business opportunities, but they don't reach into your creative brain to spawn new thoughts.

- <u>Novels</u>. They will improve your vocabulary and develop a deep roster of cocktail party conversation. Try a variety of authors. In the past year, I've read Jack London, Kurt Vonnegut, Orhan Pamuk, Oscar Wilde, Joseph Heller, Amos Oz, Salman Rushdie, and Isaac Asimov.

- <u>Research-based books and nonfiction</u>. Personally, I like reading about the human brain and decisions, economics, and price theory. A few popular authors nowadays include Malcolm Gladwell, Dan Ariely, and Thomas Friedman. Find your own niche of nonfiction and read it regularly.

- <u>Business and entrepreneurship books</u>. You're already doing that with this book. More of this.

You need not take my word for it. Here are a few articles showing the positive effects of reading:

- www.journals.lww.com/neurotodayonline/Fulltext/2010/01210/White_Matter_Brain_Changes_Result_from_Reading.9.aspx

- www.pickthebrain.com/blog/improve-your-mind-by-reading-the-classics/

- www.pickthebrain.com/blog/the-5-types-of-books-that-increase-intelligence

- www.cedu.niu.edu/~smith/Unpubs/mwera94_2.pdf

Reading List for Selling, Strategies, and Account Management

<u>The Macro Process on Sales Strategy & Process</u>

These books will start you on your PhD in the sales process for enterprise and major account selling:

- The Huthwaite Institute - "SPIN Selling" and "Major Account Sales Strategy" (www.huthwaite.com)

- Brian Burns - "Selling in a New Market"
- Geoffrey Moore - "Crossing the Chasm"

The Micro Process

- Jeffrey Gitomer (www.gitomer.com) focuses on why people buy, how purchasing decisions are made, and how to develop your personal brand. A bit of his personal branding is kitchy for enterprise sales, but you'll skim a few good ideas. I mostly like Gitomer for his perspective of why people buy.

- Brian Tracy (www.briantracy.com) recorded his audio series "The Psychology of Selling." Listen to it in your car.

- Dale Carnegie's "How to Win Friends and Influence People" covers everything you need on engaging in conversations and placing your prospect squarely in the spotlight every time. This book teaches you how to listen and the importance of "you" in a conversation versus "I/me" and how to use "and" instead of "but" in a conversation. Read this book and you'll even experience better results from your post office and DMV interactions.

Tactical

This includes phone strategies, leaving voicemails, asking the right questions, and leading effective demonstrations:

- Michael Pedone (www.salesbuzz.com) – Nobody is better when it comes to selling over the phone, leaving voicemails, and prospecting.

- Peter Cohen - "GreatDemo!" (www.secondderivative.com) – He will amaze you. If you have the opportunity to attend his live workshops, they are very, very, very good and well worth the investment. The groups are small (my workshop had ten of us) and each of us spent the day working on our own demos plus gave a presentation at the end to practice our new delivery. I employed this strategy and closed an account that had been sitting on the sidelines for almost a year in the "we're not ready to make a decision" mode.

Motivational

- Zig Ziglar is the man you want when your need a push with a side of humor to make the next sales call. Check out "The Secrets of Closing the Sale" (www.ziglar.com). He's a fantastic speaker because he talks like a normal person and injects self-effacing humor into his talks. It's great stuff for the car or the plane. You'll laugh out loud at least a few times.

- James Altucher writes "The Altucher Confidential" blog (www.jamesaltucher.com). He'll make you think about yourself, what's holding you back, and what really matters. It's a raw perspective on starting a business, taking action, and being happy. In particular, I used his "Daily Practice" idea for my own work.

Stay Inspired

I spent Thanksgiving with my in-laws at a pretty little vacation spot in Oregon. I was feeling a bit lazy, when my mother-in-law and my wife, who was five months pregnant at the time, announced they were going to the gym, so I followed. That's what it took to get me (a guy who's run marathons and finished triathlons) out of the condo and feeling good about myself and my body. Find inspiration wherever you can.

Read a blog post about someone who taught themselves Python or Ruby on Rails. Spend time watching videos and presentations about how other entrepreneurs persevered and found solutions to their business problems. Check out Stanford University's Entrepreneurship Corner: http://ecorner.stanford.edu/podcasts.html. Do whatever you have to do to stay inspired. Your customers need you to be happy, motivated, and enthusiastic. Be the most positive conversationalist your prospects speak with every day. Years ago, during my career in textbook publishing, I worked with a recruiter who always, always, always had a positive and upbeat tone on every call we had. It was truly delightful to have those conversations, because I knew I would leave the call feeling optimistic.

The Charlie Rose Show

I read an article a couple years ago about *The Charlie Rose Show* in Fortune Magazine. Apparently, Warren Buffett records every show and watches them. Good enough for Warren is good enough for me. I set up my DVR to do the same and on Sunday mornings, I sit down to watch the week's interviews that interest me. Just this week, I watched interviews with Wade Davis, author of "Into the Silence: The Great War, Mallory, and the Conquest of Everest," and Steven Naifeh and Gregory White Smith on their book "Van Gogh: The Life." Last year, Charlie Rose hosted a 12-part series on the human brain and all of its intricacies. None of this is at all related to my work, which is exactly the point. Besides, these are crazy smart people on his show, much smarter than you or me. If you don't like Charlie Rose, try TED.com. Stretch your mind outside of software, product, customers, and finances.

Find a regular resource to give yourself a respite from your day to day madness with thinking that will stretch you in new places. You'll be surprised how often you can use your discoveries in your daily conversation.

Remember:

Sales Tenet #12: Be nice. Always, always, always be nice.

12 - Love the Grind

Sales Rep: "Man, I was really busy at work today."

Manager: "Great! Lots of demos? Couple of advances? A new client?"

Sales Rep: "Not one, but my email was blowing up all day. Then the marketing team asked me to sit in on their two-hour monthly planning meeting. Then one of my customers asked me to call them so we ended up talking for almost an hour about problems they were having with their database."

Manager: "We don't sell, service, or manage databases. We're a trucking company."

Sales Rep: "I know. Can you believe it? Before I looked up, it was 1:30 and I hadn't eaten lunch, got back at 2:30 and a bunch of people I replied to in my morning emails had more questions."

Focus on your "business" not your "busy-ness."[1]

What do you notice when you go to the doctor's office? Her schedule is full and she frequently doesn't know what patient she's seeing until just before she walks in the door and grabs

Source: http://commons.wikimedia.org/wiki/File:Grind_stone.JPG

---

[1] Attribution to Jon Sterling www.linkedin.com/in/mistersterling.

the clipboard. (This part is a little troubling, but you get the point.) Your doctor, attorney, accountant and every other personal services professional has their days mapped out in advance. You need to do to the same. A couple of rules:

1. <u>Twice as long, half the reward.</u> This is a simple rule. Accept it and get used to it. The sooner you do, the sooner you'll enjoy your success. It's the sales process that you must appreciate and enjoy, not the "close." You might enter the sales process with visions of a new $500,000/year customer that ultimately will end up starting off at $50,000/year. That's okay. It happens. Be nice, focus on the relationship, and help your customers succeed. They will reward you, when they grow faster and you were a reason for it.

2. <u>This is why you must love the grind.</u> Slowdowns occur. Priorities change, budgets change, personnel changes, CEOs leave, and champions leave. People who you thought were champions really were just Vampires and Gatekeepers. It's part of the process. Smile, be nice, and keep going.

3. <u>Do NOT hire "closers" or aspire to be a "closer."</u> "Closers" hate the grind. In business-to-business sales, enterprise sales, major account selling (whatever you want to call it) you must expect and thrive in a complex organizational sales process and understand your own relationship to that process. Achieving advances, hosting on a call with the decision committee, receiving action from the client, discussing price; these are all "closes" and if any one of these fails to happen, you don't have a sale. Any salesperson that prides themselves on being a "closer" in a Glengarry Glen Ross sort of way is the last person you want developing relationships with high-ticket customers. (Recommend reading: "Trust-Based Selling" by Charles Green.) The Huthwaite Corporation studied over 35,000 sales calls and concluded that "closers" and closing techniques have zero and even a negative impact on enterprise-level sales. (Huthwaite published numerous white papers on these topics: www.huthwaite.com.)

In the enterprise sale, you're dealing with multiple decision-makers and committees (formal or informal). As a salesperson, you will be interacting with committee members numerous times over several months and any cheap attempt to prematurely close the sale may torpedo the sales process for your company altogether.

You cannot compress a six-month sales cycle into one-month just by being a "closer." Your clients are sophisticated managers (usually) that are seeking a long-term solution for a difficult business problem. The sales process requires a sales professional to identify Product Champions, antagonists, and the critical business issues to target throughout the stages of the sale.

You will very rarely find a point in any conversation where you are present to deliver a "closing line" (i.e., "It looks like you have all of information you need, so if you'll just sign here. Use my pen.") Instead, the prospect's decision is an educational process in which your sales professionalism needs to be integrated in order to earn the sale. The contract and negotiation phase itself even after the decision is made will take several calls and offer opportunities for the sale to fail. In most big sales, the line is blurred between the decision, the contract's execution, the initial payment, and an implementation phase that might last months or even a year.

Who do you want managing this process, the sales professional or a "closer" worried about when to deliver a cute line? Ultimately, of course, you want a sales professional who is comfortable with leading the prospect through the sales and contract process. This is not for the impatient "closer", but instead for a sales professional that genuinely cares about solving her client's problems.

Planning

Monday is the most important day of the week. Well, it's really Friday, because you're planning ahead to Monday. Tuesday, Wednesday, and Thursday are important because you should executing your weekly plan, gaining advances, and prospecting to set appointments for the next few days. Seeing a trend here? *Every* day is the most important day of the week.

I find that Monday, especially Monday morning, is the single best time to do outbound calls. Why?

1. It's early enough in the week that if you get voicemail that you can give yourself permission to call back on Thursday without seeming pushy. Do this on a Tuesday/Friday plan and people can use Friday to blow you off or tell you, "Yeah, just call me next week and we'll set something up."

2. Most people don't set internal meetings for Monday morning, because no one wants to start the week in a meeting. (A generalization of course.) This means calendars are clear. PICK UP THE PHONE.

3. You're setting the pace for the week and accomplishing the hard chores of selling. You'll feel a tremendous sense of accomplishment when you've had five new calls and set two demos

for later in the week before 11:30 am on Monday. Plus, think about your team walking in the door on Monday watching and hearing you on the phone tracking down business to support them and their work.

Do a Daily Practice (Also see www.jamesaltucher.com and www.tdp.com.)

This is easy. It's a business plan for the next day. After doing weekly "Sales Cannons" with the idea of identifying the three (3) major goals to accomplish during the week, I found that the "urgent-but-not-important" customer requests, emails, phone calls, and generally poor time management skills force the Top Three out of view. Now, I do a Daily Practice: "What three things/calls/accomplishments must I complete before I leave the office tomorrow?" Your time management will improve remarkably, as will your results. By making this simple list, your brain goes into high gear in the background, when you're at home with your family. It is subconsciously developing ideas, so that when you awake the next day, you'll have 3-4 new ideas to implement that day to meet your daily objectives.

The Holidays

I love the weeks before a holiday. People are motivated to get things done. It's the ultimate "poop or get off the pot" realization for your pipeline. If you call a prospect and they want to talk, initiate another call, or set up a demo for the week before a holiday, then they're interested. If you hear the "let's come back to it after the holidays" waffle, first you should respond by developing urgency. If that doesn't work, drop them down your priority list. It means they really aren't interested right now, which means that you haven't shown them enough value. This gives you the opportunity to reset the relationship and come back at them in the New Year with a fresh approach (See Chapter 6 – More Sales Process).

Prospects are also generally more affable during the holidays. They'll open up to you. They've been spending time grinding through budget meetings, strategy meetings, explaining why they missed their number this year and justifying why they are sandbagging for next year. THIS IS YOUR OPENING! Talk to them about their business.

Some questions to use around the holidays and year-end:

- How did you year end up? What worked for your business that surprised you? What didn't? Stay positive. Don't make the prospect delve into too much negativity, but do have an honest conversation with them.

- Where do you feel like you missed opportunities and what opportunities do you want to capture next year?

- What are you seeing for next year? What are your 2-3 top priorities for Q1? What do you need to do to get ahead of the curve in the next year, so you're not chasing your numbers all year?

These are all strategic questions, and more importantly, situational questions. You're learning about their business and places where they know they need improvement. You can return to them in January with specific ideas on how your products can solve their problems. If they are really in pain, help right away before the end of the year.

Schedule time with yourself to review your top 10, 20, 50 targets; take stock of where you are with them and write it down. Post-holidays, set aside 2-3 days to go through your dropped priority list and power through them. Be ready with ideas on how to grow their business. Don't do a demo of a new product. Don't talk about the new product that you just released or the one soon to be released. Just talk about their business and the ideas that you have for them. If you can't come up with any ideas, do more research before you call them.

Even if they reject your idea, it doesn't matter. It shows you're thinking about their business, that you took the conversation during the holidays seriously and you're ready for action. If they still don't take your calls, drop them back into your marketing drip and move along.

Why isn't this person/company a customer yet?

This is the primary question you need to answer for yourself. It forces you to take stock of your sales activities and answer questions like these:

- Who is/are the real decision-makers?

- Do I have a Vampire or a Gatekeeper here? How do I get around that?

- Are trends emerging of customer types that are not interested in purchasing my product?

I use this simple table for reference, filling in a worksheet for each prospect and lead to understand exactly where I am with the sales process. If you don't know the answers to all of the areas of the table, this alone could be the reason why you don't yet have the sale. Only after you know the key aspects of the process will you be able to address each.

Prospect | Company Name & Division	
Product Champion | How do I know?	
Main Decision-Maker(s) | Am I sure?	
Antagonist(s) – Who's working against me and why?	
Other Committee Members | Who could I be missing?	
Decision Phase - ie. Early stage, Committee Formation, Reviewing available options, Getting serious, I'm either in or out*	
When will the final decision be made and why?	
How do I know?	

*Check out "Major Account Sales Strategies" by Neil Rackham for more a formal structured approach to "Stages of the Sale." He breaks them into four main stages: 1) Needs Analysis, 2) Evaluation of Options, 3) Resolution of Concerns, and 4) Implementation.

Call Preps

Type out what you expect to say and where you expect to lead the call. Practice delivering what you plan to say two or three times aloud. If you have a whiteboard, sketch out a flowchart of how you'd like the call to progress. You may be knocked off course. This is perfectly fine. The flowchart keeps you focused and also identifies what you missed in this call and what you know you need to achieve in your next call with that prospect.

When you're on the phone, stand up while you are talking. You will sound more authoritative and confident.

Here's an example Call Prep that we did with a "Big Bank" account. Notice the level of detail:

Big Bank – Jim Chambers

REO PROCESS - AS DESCRIBED FROM JIM BEFORE

1. Property comes in the door

2. Goes into a valuation status - and real estate agent gets assigned immediately to the property. (VALUATION)

3. If the property is occupied, then eviction process starts. If property is vacant, then a broker is assigned to do a BPO, and then an appraisal is ordered as well.

4. Delivered back to Big Bank

5. Enters another valuation process - to confirm the value and repairs needed. (VALUATION)

> OPENING SCRIPT:
>
> "Hey Jim, thanks for getting on a call with us. I know this has been an adventure so I appreciate the time to show you the case studies that we worked on a few months ago.
>
> What I'd like to review a couple of ideas with you on your valuation process. Based on the information you provided on a few properties, I did an analysis on each using our data so that you can see how your team would utilize the data. Sound good?"

More Situational Questions for the call:

1. What goes into this valuation process?
2. Over to the Bank reps to decide on a Marketing Strategy based on $ amount of repairs needed, and when to list the property.
3. How do you decide on how much $ should be spent on the property? What factors go into this decision? Is it safe to say that there are times that the market is tanking and dumping $5000 into a rehab might be pointless?
4. Property is now listed at a price based on values + strategy decided upon by Marketing Team.
5. What factors go into the listing price? Would it be beneficial to have a complete list of all active comps in a central location that can be sorted? If you knew that the market was tanking, would that have an effect on how you price the homes? Do you rent them out at all?
6. Either they start getting offers, or have to take price reductions. At 30 days, a review is done. Do reps have the authority to reduce the price at any time?
7. How many price reductions do you do? Is there a max? Seems like having a normalized list of the days on market for each property would help forecast when these assets will sell.

SHOW PRESENTATION

[Remember to pause and ask questions!]

SET CRITERIA

> "This is just showing you a small sample set... just in California alone you have over 10,000 properties on the market. Even if we helped you evaluate and make rehab decisions on only 2% of the properties, that's already 2000 homes and assuming a very low $2000 per home, then that's $4 million we've added to your bottom line."

ACTION ITEMS

"So based on what we've covered, what should we do next?"

"While I know we're still early in your evaluation process, tell me this – how are purchases like this normally channeled and approved?"

DO NOT LEAVE THE CALL WITHOUT

- Other committee members
- Commitment for presentation to committee
- Budget & approval process

Take Call Notes

Your memory will fail you. Take the time during calls to record notes, even if you have to pause and ask your prospect, "Would you mind repeating that? I don't think I got everything that you just said and I want to make sure I understand it correctly."

Here's an example of call notes from a recent call:

Opened up call with intro from call prep. He confirmed that he was very engaged with the Bulk REO process. "Testing the waters." Said other banks have tried.

Current process is out for bidding with 2 level process – indicative bids incoming now. Investors were asked to participate. Finalizing and accepting bids now. Possible second round of bidding if needed. Can do a partial acceptance.

Choosing assets – looking at inventory, selected based on geography, condition, age Said they provide AVMs, BPOs to sellers.

He then asked about where I data could fit. Explained how BPOs are generally incomplete – 3 listings and 3 comps. Not a complete look at the market. No insight on trend.

He understood immediately – thought that we could provide 'color'. Told him that was exactly it. Said he liked the idea.

Told him we could run a pilot for his next pool. Said next pool is Feb/March 2012. Agreed that I would call him mid-January to re-engage and see where this process went. I used the term 'partnership' – said 'we've gotten to know each other pretty well this past year and we're completely comfortable running a beta/pilot w/o his bank feeling that they need to buy a bunch of data and sign a contract. He liked that and agreed. Said he knows our data is unique and useful and it's about finding a niche in his company for it. (I hate the idea that he's thinking 'niche' but if that gets us in, I'll take it.)

Summary Notes

After the call, take fifteen minutes to draft and send an email to the client that includes the three main takeaways from the call. They should follow this order:

- Bullet 1: The client's problem
- Bullet 2: Proposed solution discussed
- Bullet 3: Next steps

For example:

Hi Bill:

Thank you for your time today. We covered a lot of ground today, so here are the main takeaways that I've summarized from my notes. Let me know if I've missed anything important:

- *Despite spending $150 on a BPO for every property in the portfolio, there's continuing unease about the current market value of the property because of the lagging nature of BPOs.*
- *We discussed our "Bring to Current" product and "Listing Intel" – both could be applied by your analytics team to zero in on a real-time valuation to speed up asset disposition and initial list pricing.*
- *By Friday, you'll send me a list of 20 properties for us to review with your team on Tuesday at 2 pm via web meeting. I'll send over the meeting invite separately.*

Does that sound about right?

Looking forward to getting to work on those 20 properties on Friday. If I don't hear from you by 12 noon on Friday, I'll give you a call for the proverbial kick in the tail. Talk soon.

-Scott Sambucci

Title, My Company

me@mycompany.com

(415) 555 1212

Then, if Bill doesn't get back to you with these properties, call him at 12 noon on the dot on Friday. No exceptions. Your voicemail could be something like this:

"Hi Bill – Scott Sambucci here from Altos Research. I promised to give you a call at 12 noon if you didn't get the chance to send over the sample properties. So, this is me giving you a kick in the tail. I'll try your assistant as well just in case you're out of the office unexpectedly. Give me a call at (415) 555-1212. Scott Sambucci here with Altos Research. Look forward to your call."

Do what you promise

Always do what you promise. If you leave a voicemail in your prospecting and tell someone, "I'll try you back at 2:00 today", then call them back at 2:00 today. Not 2:15 or 2:00 tomorrow or sometime next week. This is your opportunity to unilaterally build trust and show your prospect that you are dependable. It matters more than you think.

Remember:

LOVE THE GRIND.

ABOUT THE AUTHOR

Scott Sambucci is a Silicon Valley veteran, spending more than 15 years building sales processes, developing new markets, and creating technology products for two successful startups and two publicly traded companies. Throughout his career, Scott has sold educational products, software solutions, data services, and consulting engagements to:

- Top universities, including Duke University, Columbia University, and the University of Pennsylvania;

- Financial firms, including Wells Fargo, Bank of America, Morgan Stanley, and Freddie Mac;

- United States government agencies, including the Federal Housing Financing Agency, the Department of Treasury, and the Federal Reserve Bank.

Scott leads workshops across the country to help companies and individuals improve sales performance, including a workshop at the 2012 Lean Startup Conference and regular sessions with the Lean Startup Circle Meetup Group network. He regularly teaches university courses in Economics, Finance, Entrepreneurship, and Strategic Management and recently received a "Faculty Member of Excellence" award in 2012. Scott has been interviewed on CNBC, NPR, and The Financial Times.

Scott is the Founder of SalesQualia and lives in Northern California. He is a three-time Ironman triathlete.

CONNECT WITH SCOTT

www.linkedin.com/in/scottsambucci
www.twitter.com/scottsambucci
www.twitter.com/salesqualia

www.salesqualia.com
www.quora.com/Scott-Sambucci
www.scottsambucci.wordpress.com

ABOUT SALESQUALIA

Improve Sales Performance. Sell More Stuff.

SalesQualia provides:

- Personalized advisory and consulting services
- Sales Coaching Programs
- In-person & Online Workshops
- Sales Productivity Applications & Products

Visit www.salesqualia.com to register for the "SalesQualia Insider Updates" – weekly articles, videos, and ideas to help you improve your sales performance. (Yes – of course, it's free to register!)

Made in the USA
San Bernardino, CA
22 April 2015